Country Roads

Country Roads

British Columbia & SW Alberta

LIZ & JACK BRYAN

SUNFLOWER PUBLICATIONS LTD,
Vancouver, British Columbia,
Canada

Sunflower Publications Ltd.
1426 West 26th Ave.
Vancouver, British Columbia,
Canada, V6H 2B4

Canadian Cataloguing in Publication Data

Bryan, Liz 1937-
Country Roads—British Columbia & S.W. Alberta

ISBN 0-920120-07-5

1. Rural roads—British Columbia—Guide- books. 2. Rural Roads—Alberta—Guide- books. 3. British Columbia—Description and travel—1981 —Guide-books. 4. Alberta— Description and travel— 1981 —Guide-books. I. Bryan, Jack, 1934- II. Title.
FC3817.4.B79 1991 917.11'044 C91-091487-7
F1087.B79 1991

Typeset in Canada by The Typeworks

Printed and bound in Hong Kong by Hindy's Enterprise Co. Ltd.

CONTENTS

COVER PHOTO: Storm clouds over a prairie road.

For our children,
John, Nancy and David,
who came with us.

PREFACE

Country roads are not for everyone. They are usually unpaved, narrow and circuitous. They are slow, dusty in summer, rutted in spring and often lead nowhere, superficially little more than a succession of junctions and landmarks and distances. In some ways they exist as much in the mind as on a map for they vary each time you drive them, depending on mood and background awareness, on the weather, the time of day or the time of year. They give different pleasures to different people. And they can open our eyes to the rich embroideries of the land itself, its old bones and softening contours, the rhythms of climate and season.

Older and gentler than the highways, the country roads of Western Canada follow Indian trails, tracks of fur-traders and explorers, crude roads hacked hastily by men lusting for gold. They are the routes of stage coaches, covered wagons and abandoned railways; they are roads for homesteaders, ranchers driving their cattle to market and loggers hauling timber to the mills. They have put the stamp of man on the landscape.

Of the many such roads in the mountainous corner of Canada that we know, we have chosen two dozen, some of which were included in our earlier book "Backroads of British Columbia". Over the past 20 years we have driven these roads, and many others, many times and they have always given pleasure. This book describes the roads and provides sketch maps for quick location and in this sense it is a guidebook. But hopefully it is more—an exultation. History, archaeology, geology, ecology, birds, trees and flowers and snatches of unforgettably lovely landscape—they are all stitched together here, part of that marvellous quilt of many colours that is Western Canada.

The roads in this book are not limited to four-wheel drive vehicles (we drove them comfortably enough in a family sedan) but you should make sure your car is in good mechanical condition and that you have a spare tire. Carry water and picnic supplies for few of the roads have services en route. Be prepared, depending on the weather, for dust or mud holes or even patches of snow—it lingers late in the high hills. Respect private property: the road may be public, but not the land on either side. And drive slowly: country roads are not made for speed.

The maps in the book have been drawn for general orientation only and should be used in conjunction with large-scale topographical maps which will show, not only the details of the roads we travelled, but many other roads and trails, awaiting your discovery. It would take a lifetime to drive them all.

ACROSS THE INKANEEP DESERT

Love or hate, a desert demands a passionate approach. For some it is an arid wasteland, hostile and uncomfortable; but others, looking deeper, find a tough and resolute beauty which opens and enthralls the heart. There is no room here for indifference.

Canada has several pockets of dry country that justify the desert definition and one of the loveliest lies in the south Okanagan, north and east of Osoyoos Lake, a northern finger of the great Sonoran desert that thrusts up into Canada all the way from Mexico. Forget those visions of shifting, trackless sand dunes and palm trees: this is no Sahara although there are small tracts that, within a narrow field of view, might appear to be. This is dry and sandy scrubland, bony with cliffs and boulders, peppered with gnarled greasewood and sagebrush and with mats of small opuntia cactus whose spines can pierce all but the stoutest shoes.

Why does it exist here, among the juicy orchards and vineyards? The whole of the Okanagan Valley lies in an extreme rainshadow east of the Coast Mountains and Osoyoos at the southernmost end of the valley receives an average of less than 20 centimetres of rain a year. It is only intense irrigation that allows the orchards to flourish. Cut off the water supply and the desert would gradually reclaim most of the land in the valley south of Okanagan Falls. Today though, the orchards are green, producing the earliest cherries, peaches and apricots and some of the best grapes in the province. Most of the desert has been stifled. The tiny remains lie mainly within the Inkaneep Indian Reserve beside Osoyoos Lake where 12,000 hectares preserve the landscape that was here before the settlers came. By and large it is land so nearly original that the B.C. government has fenced off a section as a desert ecological reserve.

At first glance, this desert seems empty of life for most of its inhabitants are nocturnal or secretive shade seekers, yet it is home to a variety of large mammals, including deer, bighorn sheep and coyotes, and several smaller and rarer species. Here one can find five-toed kangaroo rats, sage cottontails, pocket mice and horned toads as well as rattlesnakes, scorpions and even black widow spiders. There are also many birds, including the wary sage thrasher, uncommon sparrows and perhaps the greatest concentration of birds of prey in Canada. There are several kinds of hawks, American kestrels, huge golden eagles and turkey vultures. The latter, known to birdwatchers as TVs, are eaters of carrion and can often be seen soaring in effortless spirals above the rock outcrops.

Deserts similar to the Inkaneep exist throughout the American west, each zone with its specific vegetation and occupants, and each with its own kind of beauty. However, there seems to be one dramatic difference between the deserts of the south and those of the north. In the south the deserts burst into often spectacular bloom after the annual spring rains but in the Okanagan the rainfall is rationed throughout the year, some of it in the form of snow, and the flowers bloom not in mass display but quietly and encouragingly from spring to fall. The first shiny sage buttercups of April are followed by the softer yellow bells of the fritillary, the pale pink of phlox and the purple blue of lungwort; then comes the fuzzy blue of phacelia, the pale pink stars of the ground-hugging bitterroot and the silken tissues of yellow cactus flowers. And in hot July when you think nothing at all could bloom, suddenly from the baked earth burst Mariposa lilies, elegant three-petalled flowers in a fragile shade of mauve. September sees the lion-coloured hills emblazoned with the gold of rabbitbrush while the first frosts tinge the sumac with crimson. You can see why the desert, properly watched, is an endless source of delight.

Here it is mainly Indian country and because much of it is still in its wilderness state it preserves many traces of its prehistory. Traditionally, the east side of Osoyoos Lake at the narrows (where Highway 3 now crosses) was a tribal gathering place. Indian families came from afar to fish, gather chokecherries and Saskatoon berries, trade for obsidian and vermilion and engage in inter-tribal festivities and rituals. For those who know where to look, prehistoric village sites still exist. The Salish Indians of the Okanagan lived in semi-underground houses in winter and all that is left of them today are the circular depressions known as kekuli. And many of the large boulders on the reserve contain ancient pictographs. Those wishing to explore the Inkaneep desert in depth must have permission from the band office and would do well to hire a local guide (explorations on horseback are a possibility here). But the country road that traverses the Indian reserve is public domain and will provide a good introduction to the desert's timeless appeal. It leads in a thirty kilometre circle north from Osoyoos, beginning where Highways 97 and 3 intersect.

Osoyoos has long been a crossroads, first of Indian trails, then of fur-brigade routes. The Hudson's Bay Company brigades en route from Fort Okanagan on the Columbia River to Thompson's Post at Kamloops, often 300 horses strong, camped in the meadows at the head of the lake. After the boundary settlement, the brigades were forced to seek an east-west all-Canadian route to the coast and the main Okanagan trail was abandoned. But before the valley could lapse back into silence, gold was discovered at Rock Creek to the east and later, in the Okanagan and the Cariboo. The north-south route was pressed into service again, this time by miners and cattle drivers bringing beef to the meat-hungry gold camps. And in an effort to keep trade in Canada, Edgar Dewdney built his famous trail east over the mountains from Hope to Rock Creek, the route of today's Highway 3.

From the highway intersection just north of Osoyoos drive north on Highway 97 for 4.2 kilometres and follow the sign east to a commemorative cairn opposite the cemetery which marks the site of the first colonial customs house in the Okanagan, established in 1861 soon after the Rock Creek gold strike. The post was manned by John Haynes who later became a local judge and the area's largest rancher. The side road loops back onto the highway; continue north through the orchards, stopping to watch for activity at a prominent osprey's nest on top of a power pole by the lake's northern end. Osprey have nested here for a number of years. They are early nesters, often laying their eggs in March, and feed the young in the nest for several months.

Turn off the highway east along No. 22 Road which heads through the meadows where the fur-brigades used to camp and across the chanelled Okanagan River. The dykes along the river provide access for anglers—there are good-sized rainbows here—and the meadows give good cover for bobolink, snipe, meadowlarks and short-eared owls. Across the river the road twists beside a marshy area of former river bed and past a new log house, then goes steeply up onto a sandy hill where it branches at a cluster of old wooden buildings. These tumbledown relics are all that is left of the historic Haynes ranch, built here in 1882 with lumber barged down the lakes and along the river from Okanagan Mission to replace an earlier house which burned down.

Here the valley meadows surrender to desert. The green of the marshy lakehead and the tailored orchard rows are left behind. The gravel road has turned to sand and a great stretch of sagebrush and taller antelope bush leads your eyes up into the crags of Throne Mountain. It is here, near the desert ecological reserve, that provincial government naturalists have recently reintroduced a colony of burrowing owls. Before local ranchers successfully exterminated badgers and most of the gophers from the Okanagan, the owls used to nest in the abandoned burrows where they stood on guard, providing some local gunmen with target practice. Understandably, the local population died out but new birds have been brought in from Washington State and provided with safe birthing

A rare rainbow over the north end of Osoyoos Lake illuminates the desert section of the valley, spotlighting the delta of Inkaneep Creek.

Right: The road through the Inkaneep desert leads through one of the last remaining arid biotic zones in Canada, a world of sagebrush and stony scrubland, grazed by Inkaneep cattle.

The old church at Inkaneep village: open to the elements.

Right: the ruins of historic Haynes Ranch.

traps. The owls have seemingly moved happily back into their old territory and their numbers are said to be stable. Like others of their species they are nocturnal but when they have young they also hunt in the daytime. Look for them standing on their extraordinarily long legs outside their burrows. Do not disturb the nesting area; keep your distance and use your binoculars. The cliffs behind are home to white-throated swifts and canyon wrens.

Turn right at the intersection by the old Haynes ranch and follow the sandy road back down the valley on the eastern side of Osoyoos Lake. The marshes at the lakehead are in another ecological reserve known as the Osoyoos Oxbows. There is great bird watching here and stiles give foot access to several trails. At just over three kilometres from the highway a cattleguard and large sign mark the entrance to the Inkaneep Indian Reserve and soon the road ducks into an oasis of green shadowed by a grove of cottonwoods beside Inkaneep Creek. A little way up the creek lie the remains of a prehistoric Indian village but explore only with permission—and respect.

The cottonwoods here are home to a colony of Lewis woodpeckers, birds the size and shape of crows but with pink and white fronts and red faces. They were named after explorer Meriwether Lewis of the Lewis and Clark Expedition who also had a wildflower, the Lewisia or bitterroot, named after him. Not to be outdone, Clark gave his name to the mountain bird, Clark's nutcracker and to the flower, clarkia. It is interesting that both species of birds and both flowers can be found in the Okanagan.

Just beyond the ranch by the cottonwoods (at 4.7 kilometres) the road splits again, the right fork, really more of a sandy track, plunging deep into the desert south along the eastern shore of Osoyoos Lake. The original Indian and fur-brigade trails took this route through the valley and several boulders along the trail are painted with Indian pictographs. One outstanding example is known as "the Buffalo Man" because the little stick figure wears what appears to be the bison-horn headdress common to the Indians of the Alberta plains. John Corner's classic book "Pictographs of the Interior of B.C." gives precise directions to this and other examples in the vicinity but because they are all on Indian land they are carefully guarded and you must have permission. Some of the ancient paintings and other sites have been vandalized in the past and although all archaeological sites are officially protected by law, no-one but the Indians watch over them.

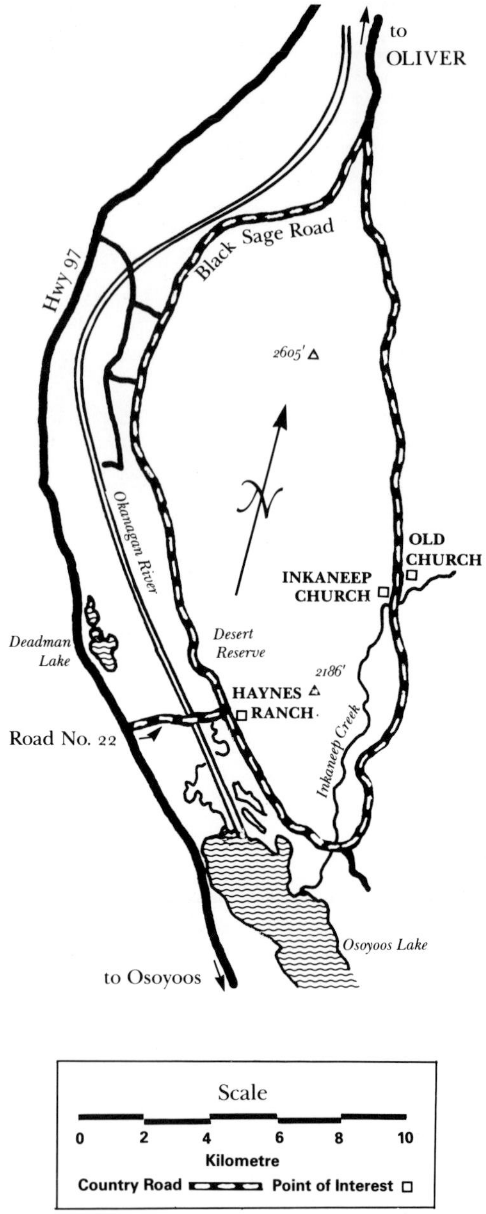

If you have permission, by all means explore these desert lands which stretch all the way down to the lakeshore and its sandy beaches and up into the dry and bony hills. Otherwise, turn left along the public road to Oliver which snakes up a draw to the east of a range of rock bluffs which guard the main valley's rim. This is prime country for turkey vultures and eagles: keep your eye on the sky. Beyond the bluffs, Indian ranchlands are green and hedged with sumac and wild clematis, a contrast to the desert hills on the opposite side of the road. Watch for California quail here.

Inkaneep village itself is scattered, as most Indian settlements seem to be. The schoolhouse appears first, then a string of houses and then, at nine kilometres, just after the road crosses the creek for the second time, the village church of St. Gregory's. This is splendidly sited on top of a bluff at a turn in the road so that as you approach it from the south its wooden tower appears suddenly against the sky.

The blue and white church is relatively new; just beyond, by the cemetery on the opposite side of the road, lies the original building of hand-hewn logs, one of the earliest churches in British Columbia. When the Okanagan Historical Society investigated in 1964 they found that the old building had been erected around an even older and smaller church. Windowless and with a sod roof, this early building was dated to before 1860. The church that was constructed around this older core was of logs, later sheathed with pine planking. Today the logs stand revealed, weathered to a marvellous red brown and the interior still bears traces of its original paint and simple altar. Open to the elements—only swallows congregate here now—its stark simplicity is somehow more eloquent of past faith than the new church opposite with its stained glass and oversize bells. The church at Inkaneep was known as the Division Church for it marked the boundary between the administration of the Oblate missionaries headquartered at Mission in the Fraser Valley and that of the Jesuits working out of Colville, Washington. Presumably, like travelling salesmen, the missionary teams agreed to stay out of each other's territory.

Beyond the churches, the land opens out to wide meadowland that in some years is planted to potatoes—a huge sea of dark luxuriant green in summer. An old weathered homestead sits in the middle of the field and one year the irrigation sprinklers watered the house as well as the potatoes, as if trying to make the old wood sprout. The road continues through fields and pine parkland, past rock bluffs and hidden lakes for some six kilometres to a T-junction at Black Sage Road. A right turn here will bring you north into the orchard town of Oliver; left circles around back to Osoyoos, this time through the vineyards. We suggest the second alternative, if only for the huge contrast between desert left as wilderness and desert made productive.

Head south, enjoying the overview of regimented orchards on one hand and dry sagebrush hills on the other. In April the gold of balsamroot sunflowers among the sagebrush vies with the colour of dandelions under the apple trees. And the antelope bush is in bloom, starry flowers of sharp green. The narrow paved road climbs and turns, revealing enchanting valley views for about five kilometres. Then the first vineyards begin: neat trellises of green stretching to the horizon border the road on both sides and stop abruptly at the northern edge of the desert ecological reserve. All too soon you are back at the Haynes ranch and the burrowing owls' nesting site, ready for another look at the Okanagan's beautiful desert.

Ironically, while the desert is home to some of earth's hardiest plants and animals, it is itself fragile. Irrigation, cultivation and the grazing of cattle destroy its long-lived yet delicately balanced ecosystem. Once erased, this can never be recreated. The Okanagan desert used to stretch from Okanagan Falls to the U.S. border; today it exists only as a tiny pocket around Osoyoos and what is left outside the ecological reserve could vanish tomorrow if more land is watered and put into production; if more suburbs are built. Enjoy it while you can.

A VALLEY FOR ALL SEASONS

The Chilliwack River Valley is a favourite destination. It is a valley for hikers, skiers, fishermen, for lovers of forest shade and lakeshore beaches. It is accessible—just a turn away from the placid Fraser Valley on good roads—yet wild enough to please those in search of solitude. If you are looking for a typical West Coast forest drive with some stupendous mountain scenery, then this one's for you, a circular route of some hundred kilometres if you go all the way to the head of the lake.

Before Europeans came to the Fraser Valley in search of furs and gold, the Stalo or River tribe of the Salish Indians lived in the Chilukweyuk (Valley of Many Streams) and here there were several villages with a mixture of housing types: the plank homes of the coast and the semi-underground pit houses or kekuli of the Interior, as if this were an overlapping boundary between Coast and Interior influences. Indian trails ran on both sides of the Chilliwack River, up the major tributaries and over the high mountain divides. American miners en route to the Fraser goldfields used the same trails and so did the loggers, who came afterwards.

A good country road, much of it paved, follows the river upstream to the end of Chilliwack Lake and unpaved forestry roads make scenic connections along the shore of the lake, the valley's northern slopes and up several of the tributary valleys. In summer there is much to do here: hiking and climbing, whitewater kayaking and rafting, boating, fishing and swimming. In winter there are cross-country ski trails and world-class steelhead fishing. In spring, when the snow has left the valley floor and buds are bursting, the mountains are at their ethereal best, thickly blanketed in white. And fall brings mist to the lake, colours to the forest and the wild bounty of mushrooms. The Chilliwack is very much a valley for all seasons. Hikers should acquire a copy of a good hiking guide for there are enough good mountain trails here for a whole summer of weekends.

The river rises in Washington State, flows into its long lake just north of the border, then curves around to run almost due west for 50 kilometres into the Fraser Valley. If you look at a map you will see that nowhere does this river flow into the Fraser. When it reaches the edge of the flatlands it has been diverted from its former course and canalized. The reformed river now flows meekly into the Fraser disguised as the Vedder, a name given in honour of the area's first settler, Volkert Vedder who arrived here in 1858.

Our explorations of the Chilliwack Valley begin in the community of Sardis. Leave the Trans Canada Highway on Exit 119 and go south for a very short way on Vedder Road. Turn left at the first traffic lights and wind your way onto Chilliwack River Road, an old trail that once led from the Fraser steamboat landing. This road is narrow and winding and leads pleasantly southwards through incipient suburbia and farm fields, in May pungent and bright with wild mustard. After five kilometres turn left (east) onto Bailey Road then veer right on Elkview

Above: Rich colours of encrusted lichens in the Chilliwack woods. Right: A newly planted section of forest along the north side of the Chilliwack River allows a splendid view of Mount Slesse.

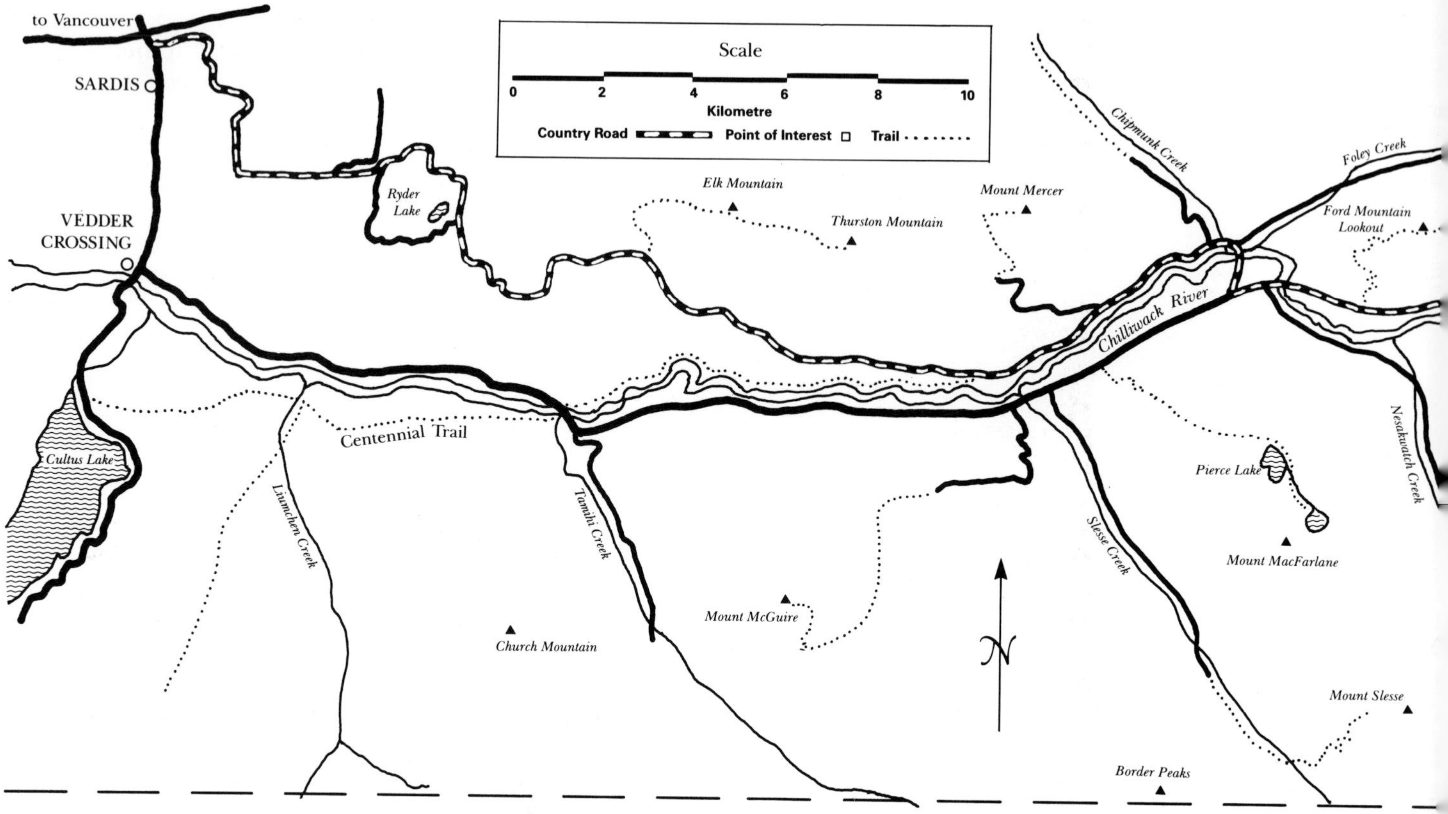

and begin a steep climb up into Ryder Lake, a pretty alp-like area poised on a high bench between the Fraser and Chilliwack valleys.

This is one of the best places in B.C. for mountain vistas. The great white peaks of the North Cascades loom skyward above shaggy fields and munching cows: the jagged sawtooth of Mount Slesse; the abrupt tent shape of Tomahoy; the crags of the Border Peaks. You can't help but lift your eyes. The area is a good one for fall and early spring walks for it is looped about with country lanes that invite casual exploration. Snow-covered, the mountain scenery all around is magnificent.

Continue along Elkview Road through the community of Ryder Lake and onto Chilliwack Bench Road, the route of a self-guided forestry tour. A "Forests in Action" Red Tour brochure available at the local tourist information centre will provide information keyed to the 16 posted stops along the way. This road is narrow and stays high above the Chilliwack Valley for about 15 kilometres before descending to river level. You will pass the start of the Elk/Thurston trail, a six-hour return trip onto an alpine ridge for spring flowers, wild summer strawberries and superb views. Make a note for a future day's easy hike.

The forests on the north side of the valley were logged around the turn of the century (notice the large size and height of the stumps) but some of the second growth trees are also huge: Douglas firs more than 50 metres tall. In other areas deciduous trees such as maple and alder are mixed in with the evergreens, a detriment to maximum timber yield but lovely to look at. With sunlight filtering through onto thick moss and ferns, the forests here are serene: a few steps off the road will bring solitude.

Along most of the northside road the trees shut out the mountain view but about four kilometres past the Elk-Thurston trailhead it passes through slopes that have been recently cleared. New Douglas firs and Grand firs were planted here in 1983 and appear to be doing well, but they are still young, short enough to allow an unobstructed view across the valley to Mounts Slesse, Pierce, Church and McGuire, and down onto the river which coils grey and gleaming far below. Slesse is Salish for "fangs". It was into the eastern fangs of

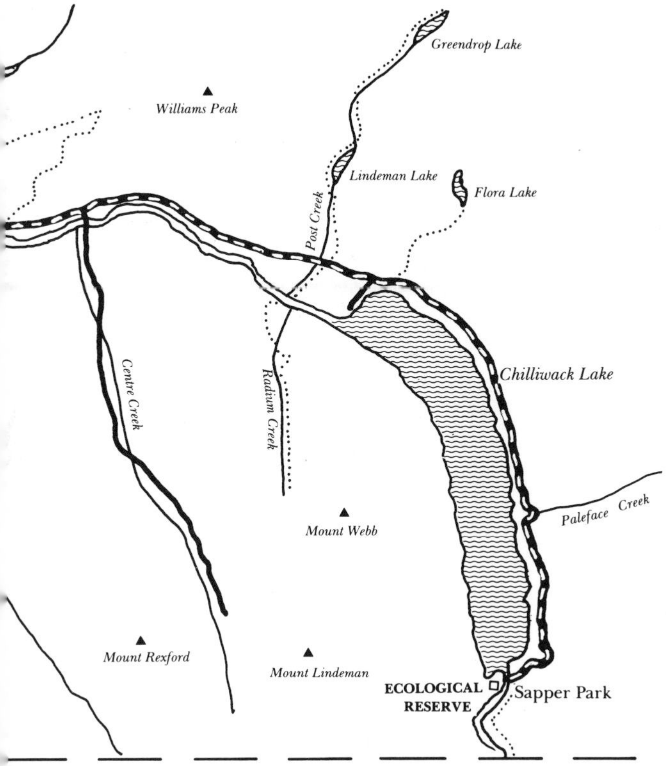

this mountain that an airliner crashed in 1953, killing all on board, including the Saskatchewan Roughriders football team.

Beyond this juvenile forest-with-a-view the road begins a slow descent onto the valley floor. In early days a logging railway was built up this side of the river and stretches of its roadbed and some traces of old trestles can still be found in the bush. Beside the river the forestry service has created several idyllic recreation sites, including Eagle's Roost, Rapids (by a churning stretch of whitewater) and Chipmunk, the latter near the narrow bridge across Chipmunk Creek, a bridge worth stopping at to take a look at the immense logs of its construction. A kilometre or so beyond the creek, the road swings around to cross Foley Creek and join the main valley road. A sideroad up Foley Creek leads to Foley Lake and gives access to several hiking trails.

From here to Chilliwack Lake, another eleven kilometres, the main valley road is wider, straighter and more travelled; in summer families head in convoys to the beach on the lake's northwestern edge. Along the way, signs point out several more hiking trails leading to alpine meadows, lakes and peaks. One that might be of interest, if only because of its multi-directional views, leads up to a fire lookout on the summit of Mount Ford. But the road is steep, the way long (15 kilometres) with an elevation gain of more than 1,000 metres. You will need a full day for this one.

At Post Creek, a series of loop trails has been designated for cross-country skiing in winter; and a hiking trail, part of the long Centennial Trail which goes all the way from New Westminster to Manning Park, takes off up the creek, past Lindeman and Greendrop lakes and over the divide into the Silverhope-Skagit Valley south of Hope. The trail to the first lake, reached in about an hour from the valley, is a good choice for a family excursion.

The wide sand beach at the end of Chilliwack Lake is a natural place for a picnic: a chance to stretch one's legs and admire the view of overlapping mountain ridges swooping down to the blue and usually placid waters. There's a large and popular campsite here and a boat launch; lake fishing is excellent for Dolly Varden, cutthroat, kokanee and rainbow. About 12 kilometres long, the lake is edged by a rough road, safely passable in two-wheel drive, which traverses its steep northeastern slope past the outlet beaches of Paleface Creek, site of a forestry campsite, and Depot Creek to end at Sappers Park at the lakehead, now an ecological reserve. Across Invicta Bridge over the inlet stream the engineers from Camp Chilliwack have built an iron gateway with plaques to denote that this was the Sappers' camp when they surveyed the international boundary back in the 1850s.

From the park, two trails head off through the ecological reserve which preserves a stretch of riverbottom marshes and virgin coast forest. The tote road the engineers cut to the 49th parallel leads up the east side of the river into Washington's North Cascades National Park and passes through some magnificent tall stands of red cedar, alder and black cottonwood. Paint markings on some of the trunks here denote "plus trees", selected for their perfect form and lusty growth. Seeds from these superior trees are collected and planted in nurseries and their seedlings used in reforestation, an experiment in genetic engineering.

Perhaps the highlight of this trail is the grove of huge Amabilis fir, a species identified by the silvery undersides of its needles. Here the trees are more than 60 metres in height and approaching 400 years old. And just beyond, within easy view of the trail, stands the largest Grand Fir on record, a giant more than 70 metres tall. A walk through the

Smoke from fall slash burning transforms Chilliwack Lake into mirrored reflections of misty blue.

Opposite Page Top: Campsite high on Slesse Ridge look out onto the high glory of the Border Peaks. Below: A field of mustard along the Chilliwack River Road near Sumas and the deep and jungled greens of the mossy forest.

jungled, untouched woods beside these neck-stretching trees is a good introduction to the glory of the Pacific Coast rainforest.

A second trail takes off upriver west of the bridge and leads through giant cedars to a stream where salmon spawn in midsummer, then heads up very steeply to Hanging Lake. Of the two trails, only the first is suitable for a casual family stroll.

For the return trip to the Fraser Valley, stay on the main road which crosses the Chilliwack River twice and passes a tree nursery, a fish hatchery and several correction camps. The large creeks coming in from the south—Centre, Nesakwatch, Slesse and Tamihi—all have forestry roads inviting one south to explore other valleys, tackle other mountain trails but this has been a long day and you might want to speed home. But stop at the Slesse bridge for an outstanding view upstream to the American and Canadian Border Peaks. The road up Slesse Creek was put in originally to service a gold mine high on the slopes of Red Mountain though now it is used for forestry access—and by climbers heading for the vertical rock walls of Mount Slesse itself. The Chilliwack's white water stretches are enjoyed by kayakers and rafters and there is a slalom course just above the lower bridge. If there is action on the river here you will want to stop and watch. Fishermen should remember that the Chilliwack, famous for its winter steelhead, is closed to all fishing above Slesse Creek.

For the small boys in your party, stop at Vedder Crossing on the way home and let them clamber on the tank at the entrance to Camp Chilliwack. And while they play here you might like to check out the museum which documents the history of the Royal Engineers in B.C. The museum is always open on summer weekends but on Sunday afternoons only the rest of the year.

IN SEARCH OF THE KETTLE VALLEY RAILWAY

The new Highway 5 which cuts across the Cascade Mountains from Hope to Merritt is a marvellous road: excitingly engineered, fast, easy to drive, and with gorgeous mountain views. Lovers of history will like the fact that it follows the route of the historic Kettle Valley Railway over the notorious Coquihalla Pass and that the old stations and flag stops, most of them named for characters in Shakespeare's plays, are commemorated along the way by nicely designed little signs. But if you look at a map, you will see that the Coquihalla Highway does not follow the route of the railway all the way. In fact, it bypasses the two most difficult sections of the route, the lower and upper canyons, joining the Coquihalla well above the station of Othello and leaving the river near Portia in favour of an easier route to the summit through the valley of Boston Bar Creek.

For fans of old railways and for those in search of slower, more interesting travel routes, the new highway's location is a blessing. The most spectacular sections of the railway's route remain intact, making it possible to explore both canyons without the harassment of freeway traffic.

The CPR's Kettle Valley Line and its epic race with the GN's Vancouver, Victoria and Eastern Railway from Midway over the mountains to Hope is a saga too long and too complicated to tell here. It is enough to say that the final stages of the contest were fought over the upper Coquihalla, a canyon so narrow and rugged that there was room for only one railway to pass through. Amazingly, in light of the years of acrimonious wrangling (including a pitched battle between railway gangs with picks and shovels) that had gone before, the two railways came to an agreement here. It was decided that the Kettle Valley would build the 87 kilometres of line from Otter Summit to Hope over the 1,100 metre Coquihalla Pass and that the VV&E would be allowed to use it for an annual fee. Perhaps the VV&E managers were scared away by the ruggedness of the terrain; perhaps they had calculated the enormous costs and guessed at the problems of keeping the line open in winter. They bowed out graciously enough and the KVR took over. At the time, the Vancouver Province reported: "The Coquihalla section will probably be the heaviest railway work ever undertaken in British Columbia". They were right. From the Coquihalla Summit to Hope, the work entailed 43 bridges, 13 tunnels, 16 snowsheds and the removal, before the days of bulldozers, of millions of cubic yards of earth and rock. The cost: an enormous $136,000 per mile, five times the average for railway construction in Canada at the time. One treacherous mile in the upper canyon alone cost more than $300,000, making it possibly the most expensive railway mile in the world. The line also proved immensely costly to upkeep: every winter the canyon was plugged by incredibly heavy snowfalls, avalanches and rockslides which closed the line, often for months at a time. Was this tremendous expenditure justified? Probably not in the light of its few years of operation. The railway opened

Above, left to right: The Quintette Tunnels of the Kettle Valley Railway in Coquihalla Canyon Provincial Park near Hope; a view down the Upper Coquihalla, showing road and railway; the entrance to one of the tunnels.

The delicate tracery of the only remaining KVR bridge in the Upper Coquihalla Canyon spans Falls Lake Creek with Bridalveil Falls in the background.

through the Coquihalla in 1916 and closed for good a scant 40 years later, defeated not only by the terrible terrain and winter conditions but by the general switch to road traffic. The opening of the Hope-Princeton Highway had much to do with its demise.

The KVR may have been short lived, but it was still one of the greatest construction feats in Canada. The engineer in charge was Andrew McCulloch, a man with little formal training who had worked his way up through the CPR construction ranks. He seemed uncannily expert in negotiating steep terrain, using spiral tunnels and long switchbacks to maintain easy grades. He saved miles of construction by cutting straight through narrow canyons and spanning yawning gulches on high steel bridges. A good example of his work can be seen near Othello just northeast of Hope where the roaring Coquihalla River cuts a deep and narrow horseshoe canyon through vertical cliffs. Here, the original railway survey called for a long bypass route and a mile-long tunnel. McCulloch resurveyed the area himself, dangling from the cliffs by ropes, and came up with a direct line through the canyon entailing several tunnels (total length only a quarter of a mile) and two short bridges over the river abyss.

These famous Quintette tunnels and the connecting bridges have been preserved in Coquihalla Canyon Provincial Park, a stop well worth making as a preamble to this country road excursion. The park can be reached by an exit from the new Coquihalla Highway, or along the Kawkawa Lake-Othello Road from Hope; the railway right-of-way through all the tunnels and over the bridges is a popular 20-minute walk. You'll quickly notice that there are only four tunnels, but one of them was "daylighted" on its north side to create the illusion of a fifth. If you can, go there during spring runoff when the river is spume-tossed and furious.

To explore the railway through the upper canyon, drive north along the Coquihalla Highway and take Exit 202 at Portia where the new highway turns into the broader confines of Boston Bar Creek, cross the Coquihalla River on Portia Bridge and drive the pipeline road. This runs on or parallel to the old KVR grade right up to the summit, a 25 kilometre drive. The road is a private one, owned and maintained by Trans Mountain Pipeline, but is it usually open and regularly travelled. Across the bridge, turn right and go by the yellow gates where a sign warns of the danger of unexploded shells from rockets used to dislodge winter avalanches. At first you are driving on the railway right-of-way but at 1.5 kilometres the road angles

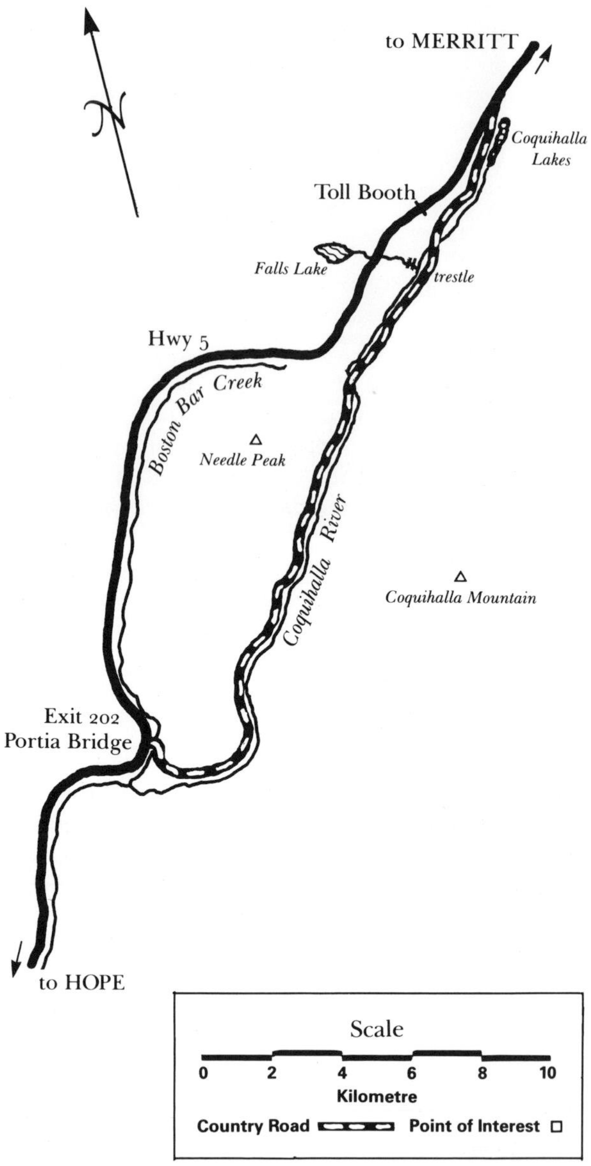

down away from the grade—if you're intent on following the railway you can hike this section—and rejoins it around the five kilometre mark. This is steep and craggy country: the railway has cut a narrow ledge along the precipitous west side of the narrow valley while the east slopes look steeper still, perpetually threatened by rock slides. The river cascades far below, tumbled with waterfalls from tributary creeks.

At eight kilometres is the hard-to-find site of Iago station where downcoming trains always stopped to cool their brakes. If you look hard enough you can find cement foundations, a red freight shed and, above the grade, a dam on the creek with an outlet pipe which fed the water tower. At 9.5 kilometres is a KVR snowshed, built in

1944 of steel-reinforced cement to replace one of the 15 original wooden sheds that protected the line through the canyon. None of these remains: shattered heaps of their timbers lie scattered down the slopes, spilled like matchsticks. The pipeline road parallels the snowshed but climbs back onto the railway grade to go through a long steel-lined concrete tunnel at 10.5 kilometres. Just beyond, across a short bridge, the rock wall above the old tracks was drilled through to divert a creek under the railway—it's an odd sensation to look into this gaping hole and see the water gushing below.

At 11 kilometres the road leaves the railway grade, crossing to the east side of the river on a bailey bridge. From here almost to the pass at Coquihalla Lakes the road is separate from the grade, though always close enough, in this narrow valley. You can see it and climb up to it and appreciate just how difficult its construction must have been. Every winter this canyon is still smothered by huge snowfalls and plagued by avalanches and rock slides. The many KVR bridges and snowsheds were regularly swept away. Along the west side of the valley, the piles of smashed trestles and snowsheds are proof of the harsh conditions. The few trestles that remained long after the railway closed were dismantled by pipeline crews for safety reasons.

The upper canyon of the Coquihalla, a deep narrow gash in the mountains, is crosshatched by the smaller canyons of tributary streams which the pipeline road crosses. The fir and cedar forests on the canyon floor are tall and beautiful. At one point you can hike in towards the railway to find huge cement pillars standing abandoned, the supports for a wooden trestle long since vanished. At about 19 kilometres you can see the remains of a bridge, a massive arch truss, which spans Slide Creek 120 metres high. All the other rail bridges here were built of timber trestles but this one, across a notorious avalanche chute, was made of steel. The bridge is intact, except for its central wooden section which was deliberately destroyed during army training manoeuvres.

The only complete railway bridge remaining crosses Falls Lake Creek at around 21 kilometres. With the creek spilling over the cliff behind in a multi-strand waterfall, this bridge must have looked just too lovely for pipeline crews to destroy. Bridalveil Falls framed by the old KVR iron truss bridge is a photograph that everyone must stop to take, for who knows how much longer the delicate wooden trestle approaches will last? It's beautiful in fall when the cottonwoods along the river are gold and the strands of the falls are well separated; but perhaps it's more dramatic in spring, when the water is a mad tumble of white. Just beyond Falls Lake Creek you can look high behind the railway to the new highway bridge spanning Dry Gulch, an equally impressive engineering feat.

The pipeline road crosses the river at 22 kilometres and runs below the railway through the increasingly narrow upper canyon which is bright in spring with great clumps of purple penstemon and mats of paler moss campion. The railway dives into three tunnels, all of them easy to reach if you care to scramble up the slope, and walking the old mossy railbed, high above the brawling infant river, is a great experience. The road climbs back onto the grade just north of the third tunnel and continues up to pavement, just south of the Coquihalla Lakes (and north of the highway toll booth) where you can easily rejoin the highway for a speedy trip down to Merritt.

Myra Canyon

A Kettle Valley Railway discovery trip cannot end without a look at another incredible and accessible section of railway engineering, Myra Canyon near Kelowna. On its journey across from the Kettle River watershed into the Okanagan, the KV climbed over the 1,200 metre pass at Hydraulic Lake (now renamed McCulloch Lake) then sidled around the hills to Chute Lake, at the same elevation, before making a short, steep and daring descent, involving a spiral tunnel down into Naramata. But the side-hill journey had to contend with the enormous 600-metre gash gouged out during Ice Age floods by the twin streams of Canyon Creek (on today's maps as KLO and Pooley Creeks.)

Even the great Andrew McCulloch was appalled at the ruggedness of this dry Interior terrain: "Never saw a railway built on any hillside such as this", he wrote in his diary and anticipated "villainously heavy" construction. His assistants advised him to abandon this route and build the railway instead along the lakeshore all the way from Kelowna to Penticton, a far longer and more costly proposition. McCulloch, however, rose to the challenge. He deftly skipped the railway around the great horseshoe bend of the precipitous canyon, employing sixteen high and curving timber trestle bridges, two enormous steel bridges and two long tunnels.

Today, all of this amazing section of line is still intact and accessible to walkers and cyclists, the high spidery trestles safe and sturdy, if a little unnerving. The terrain might seem familiar. The canyon, containing its classic example of early

Milkweed flowers beside the Kettle Valley Railway through Myra Canyon with its magnificently preserved high trestle bridges and tunnels.

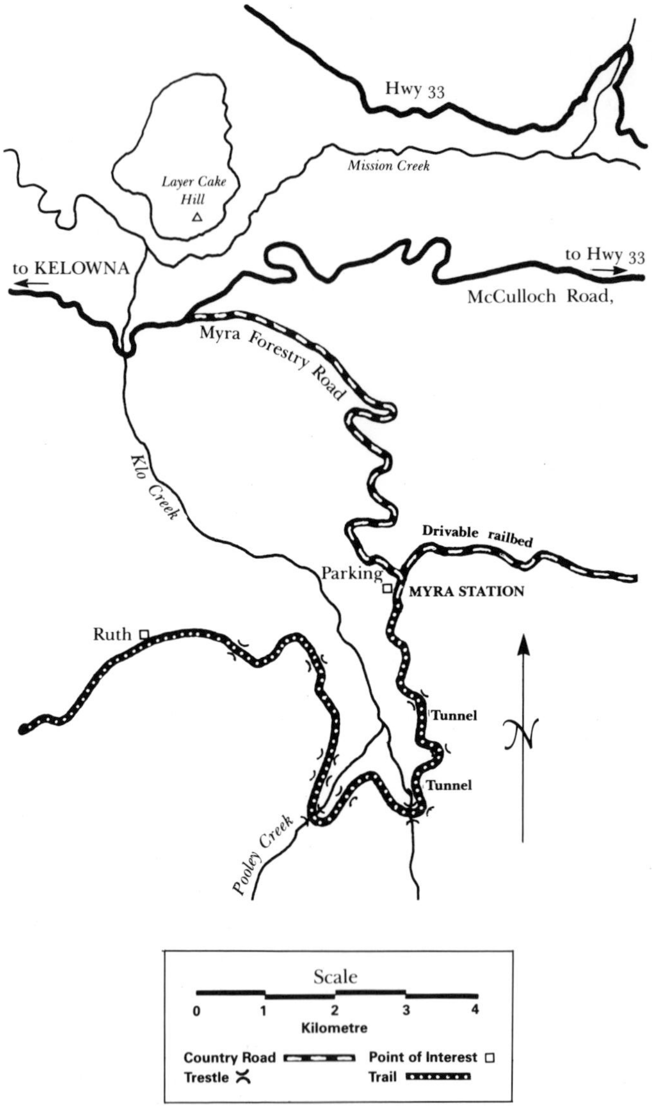

Canadian railway construction, was chosen as the locale for sequences of the CBC film made of Pierre Berton's saga, The Canadian Dream. The steam locomotive used in the film, an engine not too different from the one that made the first journey over the newly completed Kettle Valley Railway in 1916, was, perhaps fittingly, the last train through this spectacular canyon in June of 1973. When the film was completed, the line was officially closed.

To reach Myra Canyon, drive out the KLO road (the initials stand for Kelowna Land and Orchard Co.) from East Kelowna. At the McCulloch Station pub, the road becomes McCulloch Road, route of a Forestry Tour, which follows the general line of the railway over the summit to join Highway 33, the road between Kelowna and Rock Creek, just south of the turn-off to Big White ski resort. Drive McCulloch Road up into the hills until just about opposite the strikingly striped rock bluff known as Layer Cake Hill above Mission Creek canyon. Turn off uphill along Myra Road (an active logging road) and keep going until this road intersects with the old railway grade. Turn right here and drive a short way to the site of Myra Station. There's little of the station left beside foundations, but there's room to park your car here for the hike or bike ride around the canyon to the station site of Ruth.

Alternatively, drive along McCulloch Road almost to McCulloch Lake resort, watching for a hand-lettered KVR sign on the right hand side directing you down a short road onto the railway grade. Drive along the grade, an interesting experience in itself, through various rock cuts and over elevated sections until you come to the station parking site. If you miss the sign, the people at McCulloch Lake resort will likely be able to direct you. Some of the line, used as a ski-trail in the wintertime, passes through their property.

There is a move afoot to have the abandoned 500-kilometre KVR right-of-way declared a linear historic park, a hiking trail par excellence and a good way to acknowledge the important role the Kettle Valley Railway played in opening up the British Columbia interior. If every section of the line cannot be saved, surely we should not allow Myra Canyon and the Coquihalla Canyon sections to slide into oblivion. The International Bicycling and Hiking Society, Box 5, Oliver, B.C., V0H 1T0, is lobbying for the foundation of the KV Trail and would be glad of your help.

TULAMEEN STAGE ROAD

From the little town of Princeton on the rain-shadow side of the Cascade Mountains, travel routes diverge: Highway 3 plunges east, following the Similkameen River and Highway 5A, itself a little travelled and beautiful road, wanders north through Merritt to Kamloops. But there is another option: the old stage coach road which leads up the Tulameen River Valley to Aspen Grove or across to the Coquihalla Highway, a slow country road which will be a good introduction to the rich history of the area.

At first, like all of British Columbia, it was Indian country. Cliffs along the Tulameen were a source of red ochre for paint, attracting trade from as far away as the prairie grasslands. The first Europeans to enter the valley were also traders: the fur brigades tramped this way from Hope to Nicola, overnighting at Otter Lake, and they were followed in turn by prospectors who worked the creeks for gold. Later on coal was discovered and ephemeral boom towns were born; a railway came and went, ranchers came and were the only ones who stayed. Today, the settlements along the way are merely skeletons, ghost towns, if you wish to call them so, and the area has settled back into quietness.

This country road into the past begins at the top end of Princeton's Bridge Street where the original stagecoach road crossed the river that the Indians called Tulameen or Red Earth. The first settlement on its banks became known as Vermilion Forks but it was renamed Princeton in 1860 to commemorate the English Prince of Wales' visit to Canada. The steep red ochre bluffs, precious to the Indians as a source of pigment for their paint, and known to local rockhounds for petrified wood, agates and fossils, rise from the Tulameen valley floor about five kilometres north of the bridge. Geologically the red ochre is metamorphosed coal and the site is best reached by walking along the railway tracks which stay close to the river's east bank.

From Princeton it is roughly 80 meandering kilometres along the stagecoach road to Highway 5A south of Aspen Grove, or 90 kilometres across to the Coquihalla Highway. Once over the one-lane bridge, the old road (and our route) climbs steeply onto benches of open ponderosa pine, passing the access road to Snowpatch downhill ski area and the excellent cross-country trails on China Ridge. By five kilometres the road is high above the river and twists its way across steep bluffs. Newly rebuilt, this high, spectacular section provides good views into the valley and to the railway below. At 12 kilometres, the road narrows to a one-way section as it negotiates across the brightly-coloured bluffs of red ochre before swooping down to follow the river—and the railway—into Coalmont, 17.5 kilometres from Princeton.

Aptly named, Coalmont was founded around the turn of the century by the Columbia Coal and Coke Company which mined the thick seams of lignite in the nearby "mountain of coal". The railway which built up the valley from Princeton was not the Kettle Valley Railway, as one might think, but the Vancouver, Victoria and Eastern, an offshoot of the Great Northern. The American railway chugged into Coalmont in 1912 and immediately arranged to buy some 500 tonnes of coal a day to feed its hungry steam engines. Rail spurs were

Above: Evening at limpid Otter Lake.

Top Right: A display of antlers on a Tulameen shed.

Right: A blue carpet of lupines in the woods along the road to Aspen Grove.

Opposite Page: Old log buildings at the ghost town of Granite Creek. Each year more of them slip into oblivion.

built to five of the surrounding mines, but the largest and longest-lived of the mines, at Blakeburn nine kilometres up in the hills, shipped its ores to Coalmont by a 600-metre aerial tram.

When the railway reached the townsite, prosperity seemed certain. The Coalmont Courier, founded the same year, painted a rosy picture of the town's future, expecting a population of 10,000 to crowd into "the City of Destiny, the coal-mining metropolis of southern B.C." Happily for the valley, Coalmont did not live up to expectations: the surface coal was quickly mined out and deeper seams proved uneconomical. Many mines closed but the Blakeburn mine continued to be profitable right up until "Black Wednesday" of August 1930. On this terrible day, a huge explosion at the Number Four mine sealed the tunnel opening, entombing the men working underground. Rescue attempts proved futile and 45 men lost their lives—a blow from which the community never recovered. The mine reopened in a small way and continued to produce for several years; it is remembered with gratitude by oldtimers because it managed to keep going during the long years of the Depression, not closing for good until 1940.

The road from Princeton crosses the railway tracks and angles into what is left of Coalmont—a few false-front buildings along the street, several cabins under the cottonwoods and the indomitable Coalmont Hotel a large three-storey building with a long and shady verandah. The building is old and wears the ramshackle look of a long and lusty life, but it is still very much open for business.

Coal in the valley is recent history. Before that there was gold and before the gold, the long pack-trains of the fur-brigades, exhausted after their long haul over the Cascades from Fort Hope. Before Europeans discovered the country, there were the Indians. The history of the area is tightly interwoven here, and it is difficult to explore individual strands in sequence as the road blunders by.

A very short distance from the Coalmont Hotel (though a good 60 years earlier in time) lies the remains of Granite Creek, a ghost town founded on placer gold. A large gold nugget, discovered in the creek in 1885 by an American cowboy called Johnny Chance, started a minor goldrush. A prospectors' camp at the mouth of the creek soon had a population of 2,000. The camp became a town—some called it Granite City—and at one time it had more than 200 buildings, including 13 saloons. Placer gold was taken out in quantity: government reports record as much as $90,000 in four months.

Plentiful while it lasted, the fine flour gold on Granite Creek was intermixed with another mineral, lighter in colour but equal in weight, so it was difficult to separate them. Most miners did not know what this mineral was, cursed it for the extra work it entailed, and dumped it back into the river along with the worthless sand. This "white gold", as it was called, was platinum, worth far more than gold. The Tulameen River system and Russia's Amur River are the only places in the world where free platinum is found. Perhaps this circumstance has given rise to the persistent folk tale about a Swedish miner named Johanssen who did not throw away the "white gold" from his workings but kept it in a bucket. When he left the creek, he buried the full bucket near his cabin and never returned. And some say the platinum cache, an estimated ten kilograms, is still there, somewhere beside the creek, waiting to be found.

The boom times on the Granite and its upper tributaries lasted a scant three years; despite best efforts, the mother lode was never discovered and the easy gold in the creek bed and canyons was soon stripped out. The miners wandered away and the town's population thinned. One by one, the stores and hotels shut up shop, the houses were left derelict. One large extravagant house changed hands for two glasses of whiskey; another was chopped up for firewood. But the town managed to linger on, with a diehard population of optimists, for several years. By the turn of the century, one hotel and a couple of stores remained open for the 30 inhabitants. The town even survived a disastrous fire in 1907. The F.P. Cook store remained open until 1912 and as late as 1954 there were still four full-time residents.

Today though, Granite Creek (or Granite City) has little left. The river bench with its sad relics—a few sagging and roofless cabins, piles of shattered lumber, some rock foundations—is pockmarked with diggings from modern-day prospectors looking for old bottles and souvenirs—and perhaps the hidden cache of platinum. But every spring the flat is golden again with sagebrush buttercups, and gold returns to the creek every fall when the cottonwoods blaze. Protected by the B.C. Forest Service, old Granite Creek is a lovely spot at any time of year. Above the townsite lies the cemetery and rushing alongside is the creek itself, a popular and sometimes productive stream for amateur gold panning.

To reach the fast dwindling ghost of Granite Creek, turn left beside the Coalmont Hotel and drive towards the Tulameen River. The old bridge directly ahead is gone and you must zig-zag a couple of blocks downstream to cross its replacement, a single span Bailey bridge. Drive for about two

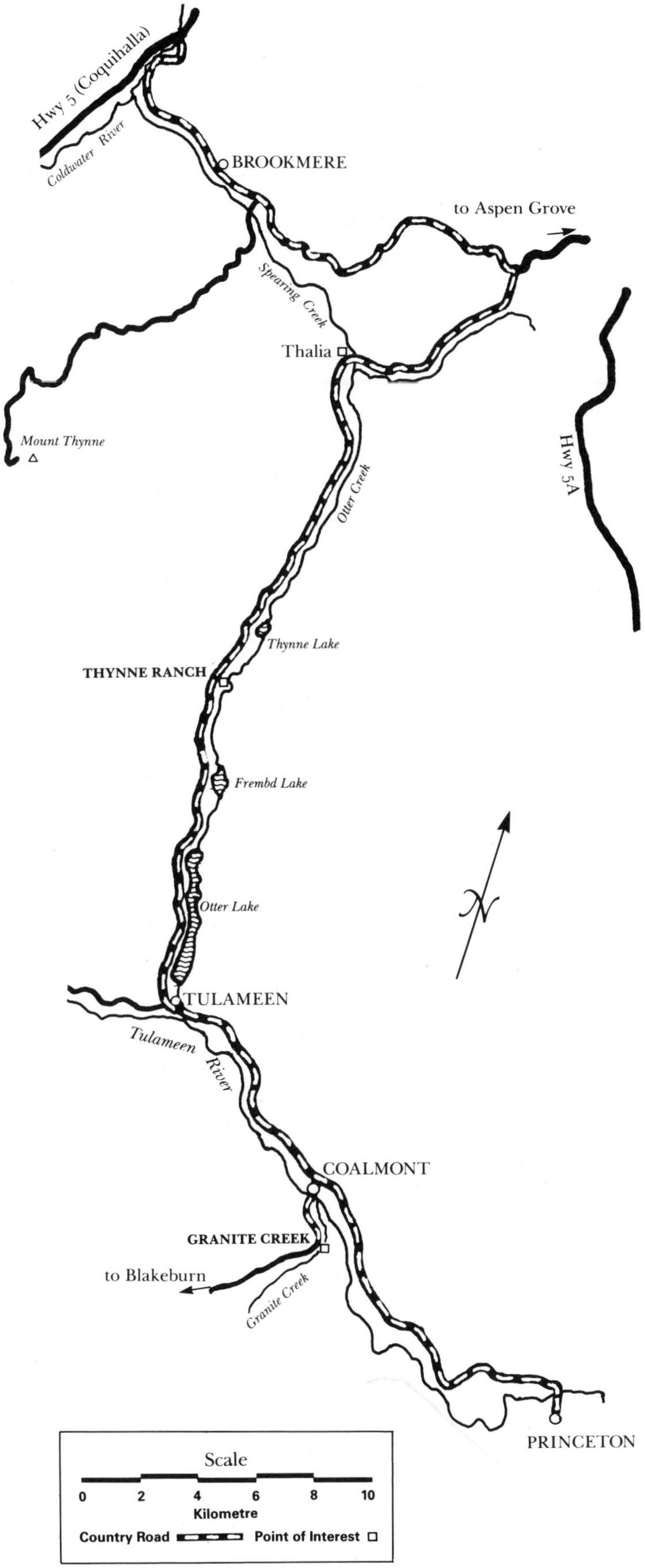

kilometres downriver to the confluence with Granite Creek. The old townsite lies beside the creek at a prominent road junction. The road that angles steeply up the mountain behind the townsite is signposted to Blakeburn, its site destroyed by an open-pit mine of the 1950s, and to Lodestone Lake on the HBC Brigade Trail.

If you look at a map, Highway 3 from Hope carves a big southward loop, following the valleys of the Sumallo, Skagit and Similkameen Rivers across to Princeton. Older trails, including the HBC Brigade trail, Whatcom, Dewdney, Hope, and an ancient Indian trail known as Blackeyes', took more direct lines across the mountains. Access to this network, much of it now marked and enfolded within the provincial Cascade Wilderness area, can be gained by continuing along the Blakeburn Road for about 20 kilometres.

Backpackers might want to head off in this direction but our country road, after dallying for a while at Granite Creek, leads back to Coalmont and heads upriver, crossing the railway several times on its way to the village of Tulameen, about 25 kilometres from Princeton or eight from the Coalmont bridge. Today's Tulameen at the foot of Otter Lake is quiet and leafy and very much alive with year-round and summer residents. There is a cafe-store-gas station here along the main street but the Dominion Hotel, for years a large, square, many-windowed landmark of past prosperity, has long since been bulldozed.

In fur trade days the site of Tulameen was known as Campement des Femmes, an Indian encampment where the women of the tribe stayed when the men went into the mountains to hunt. The brigades camped here, too, after their five-day gruelling mountain passage from Hope. And during the goldrush, a tent city of several thousand prospectors bloomed here on Otter Flats. The official Tulameen Townsite is older than Coalmont, lots being surveyed and auctioned by the provincial government in 1901. Advertised as the hub of extensive mineral deposits, with a wagon road already in place and railway connections promised, the townsite lots were soon sold out. The VV&E Railway eventually extended its line up from Princeton and began joint operations with the Kettle Valley Railway which built a spur line down from Merritt, but Tulameen never really flourished as a mining centre.

During the heyday of the railways, it was known more for its ice than its ore shipments. Otter Lake froze solidly every winter. Cut into blocks during January, the ice was shipped south to keep kitchen iceboxes cold throughout the American

The road to Brookmere, looking west towards the Coquihalla.

Opposite Page: Fall aspens along the Tulameen River at Coalmont; vestiges of the railway at Brookmere, including the shared water tower; and the overpass at Thalia in the Otter Valley.

west. The last ice shipment went out in 1925, the last passenger train from Spences Bridge to Penticton in 1964. The railways died and Tulameen station is now a private home.

From the village, a signposted road leads east up the Tulameen River to connect with the old Vuich prospectors' trail, a second access route to the historic trails system. The stagecoach road to Aspen Grove leaves the Tulameen Valley here and heads north, alongside Otter Lake, a route also followed by the railway. Bordered by the road to the west and the railway to the east, Otter Lake is a popular spot in summer for boating and water skiing and there is a commodious well-shaded campsite about five kilometres along the road. Between the village and the campsite the lake is fringed with summer cabins.

Beyond the lake the valley narrows, crowded in by steep forested mountain slopes, and a string of little lakes fills the marshy valley floor. Between the lakes, stretches of meadowland provide attractive settings for old ranches and tumbledown barns. One of the ranches is named Blackeyes, for the Indian Chief who showed the fur-traders the ancient shortcut trail over the mountains and who fed the first starved explorers with "dried carp".

At Frembd Lake, where one can troll and fly-fish for small rainbows, (and often see huge flocks of Canada geese) the railway crosses the valley and squeezes with the road against a steep scree slope, brilliant in June with clumps of penstemon. Then it crosses back again, leaving room for the spacious meadows of the Thynne Ranch, about 40 kilometres from Princeton. The trim three-storey ranchhouse stands in a shady grove of old cottonwoods surrounded by fences and barns and mountains of round-baled hay. This is one of the area's most historic buildings, a stopping place on the original wagon road before the turn of the century when the stage journey was a day and a half from Nicola (north of Merritt) to Princeton. Coaches left Nicola at 6 a.m. and arrived at Jack Thynne's house by way of Aspen Grove at 7 p.m. Here the horses would be fed and stabled and passengers put up for the night. At six the next morning, the stage left again, arriving at Granite Creek at ten and Vermilion Forks (Princeton) in time for lunch.

Beyond the meadows around Thynne Lake the road runs across steep rock scree with the creek directly below in a maze of willow and red osier dogwood, flooded by beaver dams. Where Spearing Creek flows in from the west, the railway crosses the valley, vaults the road on a wooden trestle bridge and disappears into the mountains. Near the bridge was the old VV&E railway station at Thalia, though today nothing remains. Wooden trestles like this were fire hazards, easily ignited by sparks from the coal-burning engines. Water barrels were provided on the bridges for fire extinguishers—and at Thalia these still remain. Our road ducks under the railway bridge and keeps to the north, navigating twisting Otter Creek canyon (the settlement at Thalia was once known as Canyon House) and then climbing out into a broad valley.

About 65 kilometres from Princeton, the road divides and one must choose: to follow the stagecoach route straight ahead for 14 kilometres through the forest to Highway 5A south of Aspen Grove or to turn west on the Coley Creek Forestry Road and head across to the new Highway 5 southwest of Merritt. If you choose the latter route, be prepared for a slightly rougher road, but one more interesting. About ten kilometres along, the road climbs down into Spearing Creek valley where it converges again with the railway, crossing it at the parking lot for the Thynne Mountain snowmobile trails; a side road here leads up to Thynne Mountain lookout. Turn right across the tracks and follow the railway another kilometre or so into Brookmere. This was a two-railway town, serviced by both the KVR, which came in from Merritt, and the VV&E from Princeton. Because Brookmere was a divisional point for both railways, there were two of everything: roundhouses, turntables, coaltowers, sheds and stations. The only service the two railways shared was the water tower; the spout on the north side was for the KVR, the other for the VV&E. Today, even though there are few physical remains, the railway remains the focus of attention: the tracks parallel the main street and the tall red two-spouted water tower still dominates the town.

The Brookmere station has been converted to a private house. The general store is closed, there is no school, no church or services of any kind. And yet despite its air of quiet seclusion and the small number of year-round residents, somehow the traveller experiences a sense of arrival at a place of some importance. Is this because of all the railway ghosts?

From Brookmere it's an easy dozen kilometres down Spearing Creek Valley to the Coldwater River for access to the Coquihalla Highway.

THE LONG ROAD TO WRITING-ON-STONE

Some roads are interesting not so much in themselves but because of where they lead. Writing-on-Stone provincial park is surely one of the most fascinating destinations in Western Canada. It has everything: a lovely river for swimming and canoeing; huge areas of incredible sandstone hoodoos; wildflowers and wildlife; prehistoric petroglyphs on the canyon walls, and even a reconstructed North West Mounted Police outpost. If you go there outside of the busy tourist season you will find yourself mesmerized by its magic. Indians believed it to be a place of power and it was here that the young men came on vision quests, seeking guidance from their spirits. Archaeologists think that at least some of the ancient petroglyphs are the results of these mystical experiences, scratched into the rock to give them reality. Other glyphs are the work of Indian artists who came here to record the epic events of tribal history, births and deaths, hunts and battles, a span of history that includes the coming of Europeans.

The Milk River at Writing-on-Stone is one of our favourite places. We first discovered it on a warm October afternoon when the grass was gold, the river a strand of deep blue silk and the wind malevolent. It roared in our ears and tore at our clothes, as if warning us to stay away. We were the only ones there; the campground was empty. We wandered along by the river, exploring the strange land of the hoodoos and looking at the petroglyphs. A great horned owl winked at us from a rocky perch; a cottontail rabbit nibbled on the clover. Unwilling to leave such a beautiful place, we stayed until the sun set and the moon rose over the blood-red cliffs, watching the deer come down to the river, enjoying the magic.

Most visitors travel to Writing-on-Stone by zooming down Highway 4 from Lethbridge, but such a magnificent destination deserves to be approached slowly and with anticipation. Our country road is Alberta Secondary 501 which follows the Milk River almost due east and in places straight as a die from its junction with Highway 2, south of Cardston, to the park and beyond. Once out of range of the foothills and the mountain views, the countryside becomes true prairie—huge open fields, wide horizons, an almost overwhelming sense of space and sky. The river in its wide water-scoured canyon lies far below and mostly out of sight, as it winds its way just north of the U.S. border.

Where the road leaves Highway 2, the mountain views to the west and south are truly superb. It is hard to turn one's back and travel east through the rolling farmland. At five kilometres a signpost points north to Aetna, a former thriving Mormon community right on the old Mormon Trail, the Utah settlers' route in from Salt Lake City. Around the turn of the century the little town had a cheese factory and a creamery, a school, store, blacksmith shop and meeting house; today only a few weathered log cabins remain, and these are hard to find.

Above: The alchemy of an October sunset turns sandstone cliffs at Writing-on-Stone to gold and mule deer step across the Milk River.

Right: Above the harvest shadows the hatchet face of Chief Mountain dominates the horizon west from Road 501.

The sandstone hoodoos at Writing-on-Stone above the Milk River, eerie setting for a vision quest.

Southeast of Aetna, the road dips down to cross St. Mary's River, one of several tributaries of the Oldman, which itself flows into the Bow. All these waters flow, ultimately, into the Saskatchewan and north into Hudson Bay. A few kilometres farther and the road crosses an important geological marker, the continental divide between rivers flowing north and those flowing south into the Mississippi and on into the Gulf of Mexico. One would expect such a divide to be impresssive. It is not. The Milk River Ridge (which is less a ridge than a elongated plateau) rises a scant 300 metres above the general level of the prairies and the slopes are gradual and convoluted so that at any one point the elevation gain seems minimal. Nevertheless, this height of land is an important watershed. (In Montana the continuation of the ridge is known as the Hudson Bay Divide.)

Geologists say that before the last Ice Age all the rivers in this area flowed north. When the ice began to melt, waters flowing from the receding mountain icesheet met the still solidly frozen and far more massive continental icesheet. Blocked from their former northerly direction, the rivers turned south, cutting through the Milk River Ridge and gushing southeast into the Mississippi drainage. When the continental ice drew back, the rivers resumed their former directions. The old channels scoured by mountain meltwaters were abandoned and today these form the deep, mostly dry coulees that corrugate the southern Alberta landscape. But the Milk River itself, cut into a deep canyon, continued to run southward, the only river in Alberta to flow into the Gulf of Mexico.

As you drive along you can see the low line of the Milk River Ridge to your left. But don't neglect to look often over your right shoulder: the view of the Rockies across the fields is still sensational. About 25 kilometres, the road angles sharply east and heads for the largest of the meltwater cuts in the Milk River Ridge, a lonely spot known as Whiskey Gap, once a major liquor distribution centre. The whiskey was smuggled north across the border by mule team and packhorse up from Fort Benton en route to the whiskey traders' forts around Lethbridge. This illicit trade with the Indians was stopped (or at least severely curtailed) when the North West Mounted Police came west to establish Fort Macleod and a string of border outposts. During the Prohibition Era whiskey flowed again across the border, this time from Canada into Montana. There's nothing much left now of the Whiskey Gap community; the Canadian Pacific branchline has been taken up, the huddle of grain elevators dismantled. Only a few houses remain,

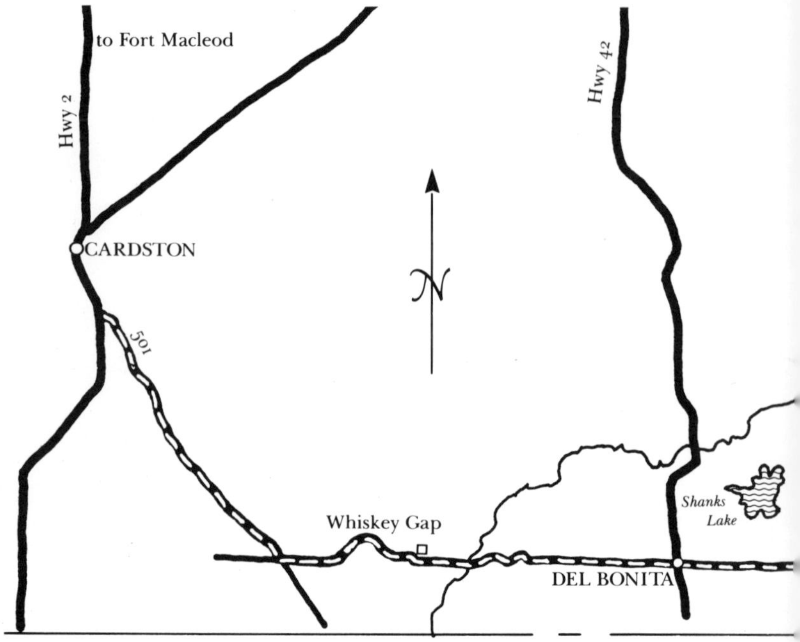

one of which has incorporated a small church into its remodelling.

Through Whiskey Gap (abstemious citizens once tried to change its name to Fareham) the road enters into Milk River drainage, though the tiny creeks that come down from the ridge and from slightly higher land to the south are difficult to see. Four kilometres from the Gap, the road crosses the beginning stream of the North Milk, then hefts itself up onto the plateau, past a picturesque ranch, an old schoolhouse, tumbledown barns, abandoned trucks and other signs of a more populated past en route to Del Bonita. Traditionally cattle range, some of the land around here has been turned over to huge flocks of sheep.

The settlement of Del Bonita at 45 kilometres has a Spanish sounding name, an interesting coincidence because this part of Alberta was once claimed by Spain as part of her American lands which included all the territory drained by the Mississippi River. It means "of the beautiful" which could be descriptive of the country though oldtimers seem to think it was called after the French saint Bonita and that del referred to the dell or valley of nearby Shanks Creek. The community today has a church, a general store and post-office and it sits astride Highway 62 three kilometres north of the customs crossing to Cutbank, Montana. Road 501 is a long and lonely one: if you're in need of sustenance, the store keeps a coffee pot hot for wayfarers.

The low dark line of the Milk River Ridge rises to the north and to the southeast the blue humps of the Sweetgrass Hills far away in Montana interrupt

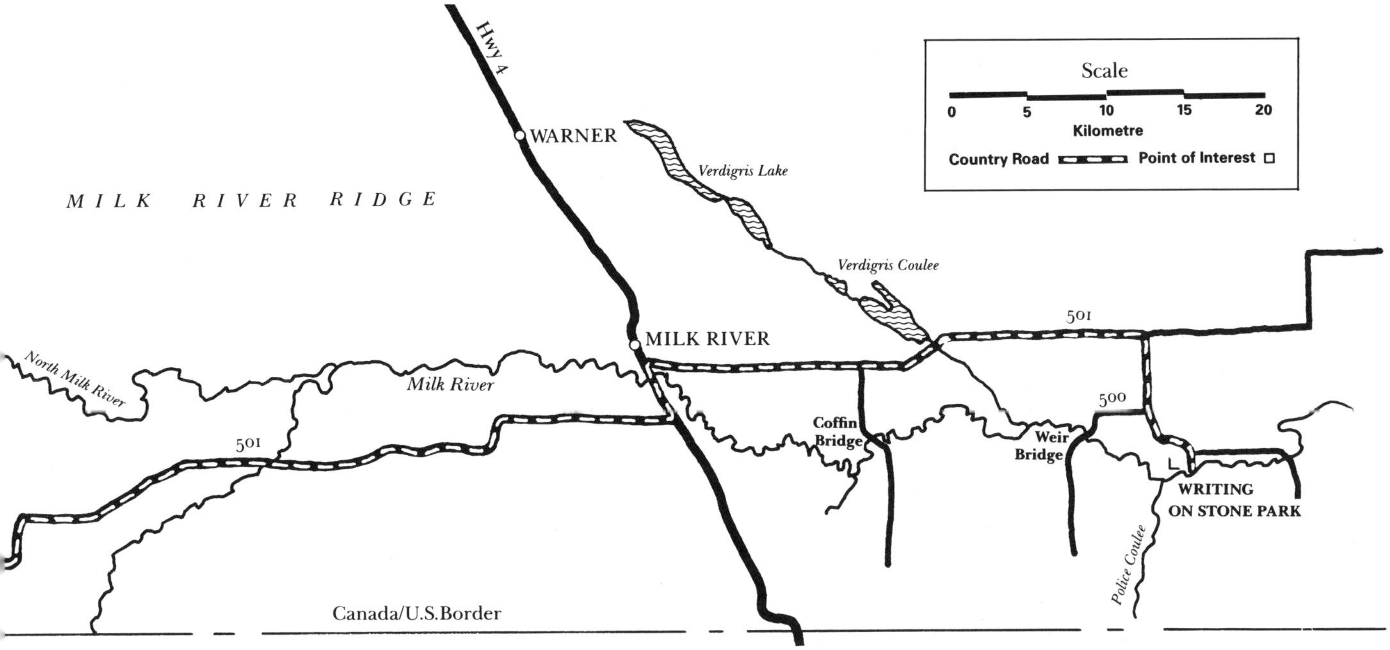

the horizon line. Rising a good thousand metres above the plains and dark with forests of Douglas fir they are striking landmarks. To the Metis buffalo hunters they were known as the Trois Buttes because there are three main blocks, all with abrupt conical summits suggestive of volcanoes. But these hills are geologic oddities, masses of once deeply buried igneous rocks uncovered during regional uplift and by the erosion of overlying materials. High and sturdy, they were never covered by the glaciers: the icesheets merely flowed around them, leaving the peaks untouched. This far away, the hills give little indication of their size and beauty. In fact, they disappear behind the horizon for most of the way.

The road east from Del Bonita meanders through arid grasslands suitable mainly for grazing. All this country was once included in Palliser's Triangle, land that John Palliser, leader of the 1857 British North American Exploring Expedition, considered unfit for settlement because of low rainfall and lack of timber. There is some cultivation on the slopes of the Milk River Ridge but basically Palliser's opinion was correct. A few hopeful homesteaders tried once to tame the land but years of drought led quickly to disappointment. Today, from here to the Saskatchewan border, it is virtually unbroken prairie still, ranged not by the buffalo of old but by cattle and sheep. And by herds of wild pronghorn antelope.

At 70 kilometres, the road swoops down to cross the Milk River, named by Lewis and Clark in 1805 because its waters were milky with silt. Here in the green valley is the Oasis Ranch; there's an interesting old silo and shed beside the road and river cliffs that are home to a swarm of swallows and their gourd-shaped nests. Twenty kilometres farther the grain elevators of the town of Milk River come into view and once again the Sweetgrass Hills pierce the horizon. Road 501 joins Highway 4 just south of the town. Turn north and cross the Milk River again, by the Government of Alberta Interpretive Centre. The parking lot here is overlooked by replicas of the sandstone hoodoos and a huge model of a dinosaur; inside, the displays take the form of a time journey through Alberta. It's well worth a stop.

From the town of Milk River, 501 heads east again, keeping to the flat prairie just north of the river which here begins to eat deeply into the bedrock, incising a canyon that in its easterly reaches is the deepest of any in the Canadian prairies. Driving along through the flatlands, however, one has no inkling of the spectacular beauty of the river in its wide meltwater valley for it lies well below the prairie level. And until you reach Writing-on-Stone Park, the only river views possible are from one of two road bridges. The first of these, ominously named Coffin, is reached from a road some 14 kilometres east of Milk River village. It is possible to drive south here, cross the river, pick up another east-going road and cross the river again on the Weir Bridge. Both these bridges are good access points for boaters: canoeing the Milk is a popular pastime because the river is gentle, the weather co-operative and the scenery grand. By the time we reach this point, we are usually eager to reach Writing-on-Stone and have no patience for side

Sandstone cliffs at Writing-on-Stone contain the largest single concentration of prehistoric Indian petroglyphs in Canada. Left: Shield-bodied warriors and a woman giving birth.

Above: The North West Mounted Police post guards the ford across the Milk River; on the skyline, the buffalo humps of the Sweetgrass Hills.

Left: The sandstone hoodoos are fretted with holes and caves and arches, a playground for kids of all ages.

Right: The prairie of southeastern Alberta, much of it unbroken, is home to large herds of pronghorn antelope.

trips, although we always stop at Verdigris Coulee, a huge former meltwater channel about three kilometres past the Coffin Bridge turnoff. The intermittent lakes here are worth scanning for white pelicans and other birds. And if you know where to look, there are Indian petroglyphs on the sandstone cliffs edging the coulee. Secondary Road 877 comes in from Skiff in the north and then 140 kilometres from the beginning of the trip another sideroad turns south to Writing-on-Stone. Nothing can fully prepare you for the first incredible view of the Milk River valley and its forest of stone hoodoos, overlooked from the south by the beautiful Sweetgrass Hills. If you are not camping overnight in the shade of the cottonwoods beside the river, make sure you allow plenty of time to explore the park, perhaps go for a swim in the clean but silty river, scramble through the hoodoos, walk the nature trails—and best of all take a guided walk into the protected archaeological preserve to see the petroglyphs and visit the restored police outpost.

Though canyon walls along other stretches of the Milk River contain smooth slabs suitable for the carving of Indian glyphs, only a few of these were used by prehistoric Indians. Most of the petroglyphs lie within park boundaries, today the largest and most important concentration of Indian rock art in Canada, a pictorial record that stretches back into prehistory at least 300 years.

On these sandstone bluffs are pictures of the nomad peoples of the plains in the days of buffalo plenty, when they fought on foot with spears and bows and arrows and carried giant shields; of the first guns and horses; of the coming of Europeans with their hats and wagons, liquor, forts and gallows. These enigmatic links to our Indian heritage can be dated roughly by the different artistic traditions and by the appearance of the horse and gun which reached Alberta only in the mid-18th century. Since their discovery by European settlers some 140 years ago, the Indian carvings have been scandalously vandalized and this is why most of them now lie within the protected archaeological preserve, closed to the public except for guided tours.

When you see the curious rocks at Writing-on-Stone you can understand why the Indians made this a sacred place. The soft sandstone formations of the cliffs, topped by thin layers of harder ironstone, have been eaten away by water and wind into weird and fanciful contortions, full of holes and arches, caves and pinnacles. The hoodoo formations provide nesting sites for great horned owls, prairie falcons and golden eagles as well as smaller kestrels. Other niches and fissures hide the nests of pack rats and rattlesnakes, the holes of marmots and cottontail rabbits. In spring and early summer, the wildflowers are varied and plentiful. It's a great place for exploration.

The first Europeans in the park were policemen, a detachment of North West Mounties who built a log outpost beside the main Blackfoot Trail to the south. Established to keep out U.S. whiskey traders and to watch for horse thieves and Indian troubles, the police post at Writing-on-Stone soon became more involved with keeping American cattle from straying north of the unfenced border, then closed for good. Recently, the old police buildings on the south side of the river have been reconstructed and refurbished in period style. To reach them, participants of guided tours must wade across the river at the old Blackfoot ford.

Secondary Road 501 continues east from Writing-on-Stone all the way to the Saskatchewan border, crossing the southern arm of intermittent Pakowki Lake, one of the largest lakes in Alberta and an excellent spot for bird watching (nesting cormorants, night herons and white-faced ibis), traversing the pronghorn grazing preserve and providing access to the Milk River Canyon and the badlands of the Lost River. But this is a separate journey, one that needs another day, another frame of mind—and a good pair of hiking boots. Our country road ends at Writing-on-Stone, where, without a doubt, you will want to stay.

OVER DOUGLAS LAKE RANGE

The hill country east of the Nicola Valley is among the country's loveliest, an undulating sweep of grassland, lupine blue in early summer, with little lakes and drifts of trees in the hollows and a great sense of space and sky. On ripe summer evenings, when the valley below is already in shade, up here the grass is golden in the sunset, the shadows long and the rounded curves of the hills have a slumbering, human aspect. Meadowlarks trill their rich warm songs and along the meandering ranch roads a scurrying army of horned larks is forever in retreat. Once blanketed with bunchgrass "higher than a horse's belly" the hills provide superb natural range for cattle.

In the heart of this lovely country lies Douglas Lake Ranch, one of Canada's largest and richest, named for John Douglas, a Scottish miner who homesteaded the first ranch holdings here in the 1870s. A subsequent owner, J.B. Greaves, can be credited with the ranch's growth. He ran a syndicate which cornered the market on Interior beef and later won the contract to supply beef to the thousands of construction workers building the Canadian Pacific Railway. The first to ship cattle out on the new railway, Greaves and his partners built a cattle empire on Nicola grasslands, gradually buying out their neighbours' holdings until today the ranch covers more than a million acres.

Across the great sweep of Douglas Lake lands runs a lovely country road which travels from Quilchena across the highlands and down into the North Okanagan at Westwold, a leisurely hundred kilometre jaunt. Interestingly, the final chapters of two of B.C.'s outlaw stories—of train robber Bill Miner and the Wild McLean Boys—were written here.

Leave the Coquihalla Highway at Merritt and take Highway 5A north, the old road through the Nicola Valley. First stop must be the settlement of Nicola, once the largest and most important town in the valley. Early in 1894 the CPR had promised to build a branch line up the Nicola River from Spences Bridge and Nicola naturally thought of itself as the terminal city. Real estate entrepreneurs planned accordingly. And 16 kilometres up the lake, today seemingly in the middle of nowhere, the grand Hotel Quilchena was built, for it seemed certain that the railway would continue up the valley to Kamloops. The railway kept its construction promise all right but built up the Nicola no farther than the upstart settlement of Forksdale at the mouth of the Coldwater River, close to newly discovered coal deposits. Forksdale was renamed Merritt after the local railway contractor and the new town blossomed while Nicola went to seed. Though people live here still, it is only a shadow of a town. There are no gas stations, no motels, no shops, nothing to hamper the turn-of-the-century atmosphere. Prominent among the old landmarks is St. Andrew's United Church built in 1876, a di-

Billowing grassland and huge skies on the high plateau near Minnie Lake, a heady experience.

Top: Abandoned irrigation flume once watered Minnie Lake pastures. Below: Douglas Lake general store.

minutive frame building painted a spanking white with a jaunty belfry. Its graveyard with leaning Victorian headstones of carved white marble is worth a visit—as are all graveyards if you have a feeling for history and the continuity of things. Opposite lies a turreted "Gothic" mansion hiding behind a lilac hedge and farther along the road is the old courthouse, its once imposing driveway now a family lawn. It's a photogenic spot.

Nicola, the river, lake and town, were named after local Indian chief N'Kwala born in the 1780s. John Tod, Hudson's Bay Company trader at Kamloops, described him as "a great chieftain and a bold man for he had seventeen wives". The lake, one of the deepest in B.C., begins at the northern edge of the old town and it is well stocked with trout, kokanee and whitefish. It is currently popular with windsurfers and there is a provincial campsite, Monck Park, on the lake's steep western side. About 4.5 kilometres north from the campsite along a rough road lies a large granite outcrop with Indian pictographs, one showing a human figure with long braids.

The highway passes along Nicola Lake's eastern shores bringing travellers to the doorstep of the three-storey Quilchena Hotel, still very much open for business during the summer months and still retaining most of its grand Victorian furnishings. Here you can sleep in a choice of old-fashioned bedrooms, including a bridal suite and the ladies' parlour, socialize in a drawing room complete with over-stuffed sofas and a square grand piano, exercise your elbows at the original bar (look for bullet holes) and dine in style. The hotel offers golf, tennis and horseback riding but no air-conditioning, television or private baths.

Adjacent to the hotel is a gas station and general store where you can pick up a Stetson, bluejeans and other cowboy paraphernalia for the hotel's owner, Guy Rose, also runs a large ranch, the Quilchena Cattle Company. Ranch cowhands are fed in the coffeeshop and behind the hotel are capacious barns and machinery sheds. If you want to stretch your legs here, walk up the road that leads from the hotel along Quilchena Creek to the stables, keeping an eye out for nesting long-billed curlews and bobolinks.

The country road across the range leaves the highway about two kilometres north of the hotel. Watch for a cattle guard and a road leading off to the east, signposted to Minnie, Paradise and Pennask Lakes. If you looked at the pages of the turn-of-the-century guest book that decorate the walls of the Quilchena Hotel, Minnie Lake will be familiar as the home of the three Raspberry brothers, frequent visitors in the hotel's early years, whose ranch was later acquired by Douglas Lake. The road climbs steeply up the dry hillside, peppered with sagebrush and cactus and in August the yellow plumes of rabbit brush. Soon there's a fine view down to the great U-shaped glacial trough filled by Nicola Lake.

If when you left the highway you expected, as many people do, to climb up into forests like those that clothe the Okanagan hills, the wide open grasslands on the top will be a revelation. Here on the western rim of the plateau about 16 kilometres from the highway, the road becomes a narrow ribbon winding through huge stretches of open meadowland, only lightly sprinkled with ponderosa pine and Douglas fir. Here among the flowers and the larks the sky suddenly seems immense. Of course the grasslands do not go on for ever. If you look eastwards from one of the rises you can see the dark line of the forests approaching; drive further east and you will be immersed in them.

Up on this high and heady plateau there are many little lakes, all of them home to nesting waterbirds and most of them well stocked with fish. Minnie and nearby Stoney lakes are on Douglas Lake Ranch property and fishing here is controlled. Fly fishing only is allowed and there is a catch limit of one fish per day. For current information about fishing or camping here, contact the Douglas Lake General Store. There are always great rafts of ducks on the lakes and usually clouds of mosquitoes. But under the eaves of an old shack beside the lake a large chittering colony of cliff swallows build their clay nests and swallows are mosquito eaters beyond compare.

Follow the road to Minnie Lake and veer left. (The road ahead, well marked, leads to Minnie Lake Ranch). Soon you will come to another junction: right the road is signposted to Pennask and Paradise Lakes. Until the building of the Okanagan Connector from Merritt to Peachland this road provided the only cross-over route from the Nicola to the central Okanagan, though you needed a four-wheel drive to accomplish this comfortably. Keep left here and follow the road across the top of the Commonage Reserve (land originally set aside to be used for grazing by both Indians and white settlers) past hayfields and duck-filled ponds to Douglas Creek which leads steeply down to Douglas Lake, about 16 kilometres from Minnie. In spring the road here might well be wet and muddy.

As soon as you begin the descent you can look down into the narrow valley of the Nicola River. The Indian village of Spahomin is marked by the

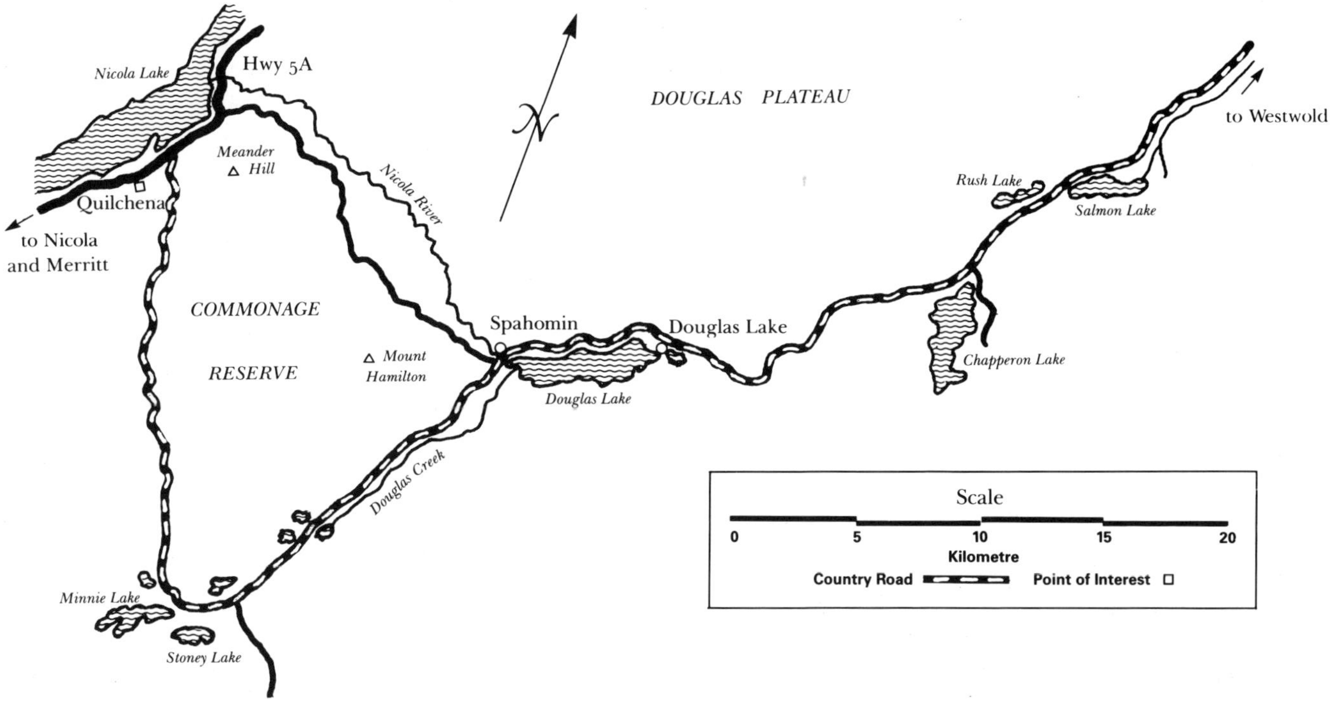

1889 wooden church of St. Nicholas, a stern little building seemingly overwhelmed by its tall tower and steeple. As you near the village, keep an eye out for old log cabins. One of them near here was the end of the line for the McLean boys who had murdered Constable John Ussher up near Kamloops and were on the run. They holed up in one of the cabins beside the creek where they were surrounded by a posse of ranchers. Hopelessly outnumbered, and after a long siege and a couple of wild west gun fights, the boys surrendered and later all four went to the gallows at New Westminster. The cabin, if it still exists, has not been identified. Make your own choice.

At Spahomin the Minnie Lake road meets the main route through Douglas Lake. A left turn here will bring you back to Highway 5A so turn right and head along the north shore of the lake, watching out for ospreys which can often be seen fishing here. Near the head of the lake is a campsite at Prince Philip's Point, named to commemorate his week-long visit to the ranch in 1962.

If you make this trip in high summer, chances are that so far you haven't seen even one cow, let alone the great beef herds of Douglas Lake. In late spring, after all the cows have given birth, they are driven to the moister grasses and forest shade of the hills around Aspen Grove and the ranch turns its attention to raising hay to feed them when they return in the fall. But there are newcomers to the grazing land here: herds of domesticated deer, raised for venison. Douglas Lake Ranch is one of at least two in southern B.C. that is raising European fallow deer, a species far smaller than our own white-tails and mule deer, and much in demand by specialty restaurants. Look for them in the meadows at the head of the lake, protected by high fences and "No Shooting" signs.

Nearby lies Douglas Lake headquarters or Home Ranch, a miniature village in itself, with houses, a school, post office, barns, workshops and storage sheds and a great little general store that has been in operation in the same two-storey frame building since the early 1900s. Home Ranch lies on the edge of a small round lake called Sanctuary, and the view across this water to the red-roofed barns against the grassy hills is peaceful, indeed. At the top end of Sanctuary Lake, the road crests a little hill and rides along a flat bench beside the ranch airstrip, crosses the creek by an old log barn and extensive corrals and wends its way northeast across the hayfields to Chapperon Lake.

It was somewhere near here that Bill Miner, American highwayman turned train robber, was tracked down by Constable William Fernie and apprehended by a mounted police posse. Miner and his two friends who had held-up and robbed the mighty CPR at Ducks, east of Kamloops, had stopped for lunch and were sitting around a campfire beside the trail. Miner, cool as a cucumber, explained that they were prospectors out from Grand Prairie (today's Westwold) but one of the others panicked and ran away, madly firing his revolver. The game was up. Miner and the others

were transported to Nicola by wagon—there's a fine old picture showing them outside the Quilchena Hotel—and thence to Kamloops for trial. One version of the tale of notorious Bill Miner was told in the movie "The Grey Fox".

The road barely touches the top end of Chapperon Lake then dives briefly into woodland for its journey across the divide and into Salmon River drainage. On the west lies Rush Lake, shallow and reedy and noisy with birdlife and to the east, a little farther on, lies Salmon Lake whose waters are open to fly fishing only (rainbows to 2 kg.) The road follows Salmon River across the plateau, passing a succession of old barns, a sturdy log house, snake fences and miscellaneous ranch buildings, all showing signs of weather. Here lies the most northerly tract of the Douglas Lake empire, the old ranch holdings of Owen Batchelor, now known as Batchelors Meadows. As the road drops steeply down towards the river canyon, the grasslands are left behind and the horizon closes in. There's a forestry campsite tucked under the trees and the road becomes narrow and winding before it bursts out above a little box valley, with green fields and grazing sheep, for the last leg of the trip to Westwold and Highway 97 to Kamloops.

It was at a ranch in the gentle valley at Westwold that the last of the Cariboo camels, brought in for hauling supplies on the road to the goldfields (an experiment that failed), lived out its days, expiring finally in 1905 after years of exile in a cold foreign land.

Opposite Page: Douglas Lake Home Ranch across Sanctuary Lake.

Top, left to right: The grand old Quilchena Hotel and the green valley of the Nicola; boats at Minnie Lake.

THOMPSON RIVER ALTERNATIVE

From Kamloops the Trans-Canada Highway on the south side of the Thompson River dashes east 60 kilometres to the village of Chase. It's understandably a busy road with few opportunities to stop and enjoy the scenery. But on the other side of the river, there's a quiet country route that covers much the same distance, but oh! so much more leisurely. Here you can loiter all you like, and that's what country roads are for.

To find this quiet road, drive across the river on Highway 5, the Yellowhead route to Jasper. Shortly after the bridge, turn right (east) on Shuswap Road just past the red brick buildings of the former Indian residential school built in 1889 and now the Secwepemc museum and Indian band office. Almost at once you are away from the bustle of highways and into the silent sagebrush, dry and dusty in summer, with the noise of the highway on the opposite shore only a muffled roar. There's time now to watch the flycatchers in the cottonwood trees along the river or take photographs of the milkweed in bloom.

Highway travellers see only from afar the great eroded clay cliffs across the river. But the north side country road leads right under them, and what fantastic castle shapes they are, fretted by wind and rain and slashed with deep canyons. They date from the melting days of the Ice Age, when sedimentary deposits from the hills sluiced down into a valley still choked with stagnant ice, but a scientific explanation doesn't make them less spectacular. Drive by them slowly and stop often. At roughly ten kilometres from the highway, a side road leads a short distance up a gulley right under some of the most interesting castle shapes, a perfect spot for a picnic or for careful explorations on foot. Between the cliffs and the surging silk of the river lie long fields of alfalfa, pungent in places with sharp yellow clouds of wild mustard. Where irrigation stops, sagebrush and desert weeds return. The contrasts are exhilarating.

A little farther on, a side valley with a "No Through Road" sign leads through a sandy draw to the old Harper Ranch, founded in 1862. Here Thaddeus and Jerome Harper raised beef and sent it on the hoof to feed the gold camps of the Cariboo. The brothers went on to found the famous Gang Ranch of the Cariboo and it was a subsequent ranch owner who damned Paul Creek in the hills behind, to form a storage lake for irrigation. The Paul Lake reservoir is now a provincial park popular for its beaches, boating, fishing and commodious campsite.

By 16 kilometres, the clay cliffs have disappeared and a cement works strikes a discordant note in an otherwise harmonious landscape. If you must return to the highway, there's a bridge here. East for several kilometres the quiet side of the river has been adopted by houses, a golf and country club and a turf ranch. At 24 kilometres, the

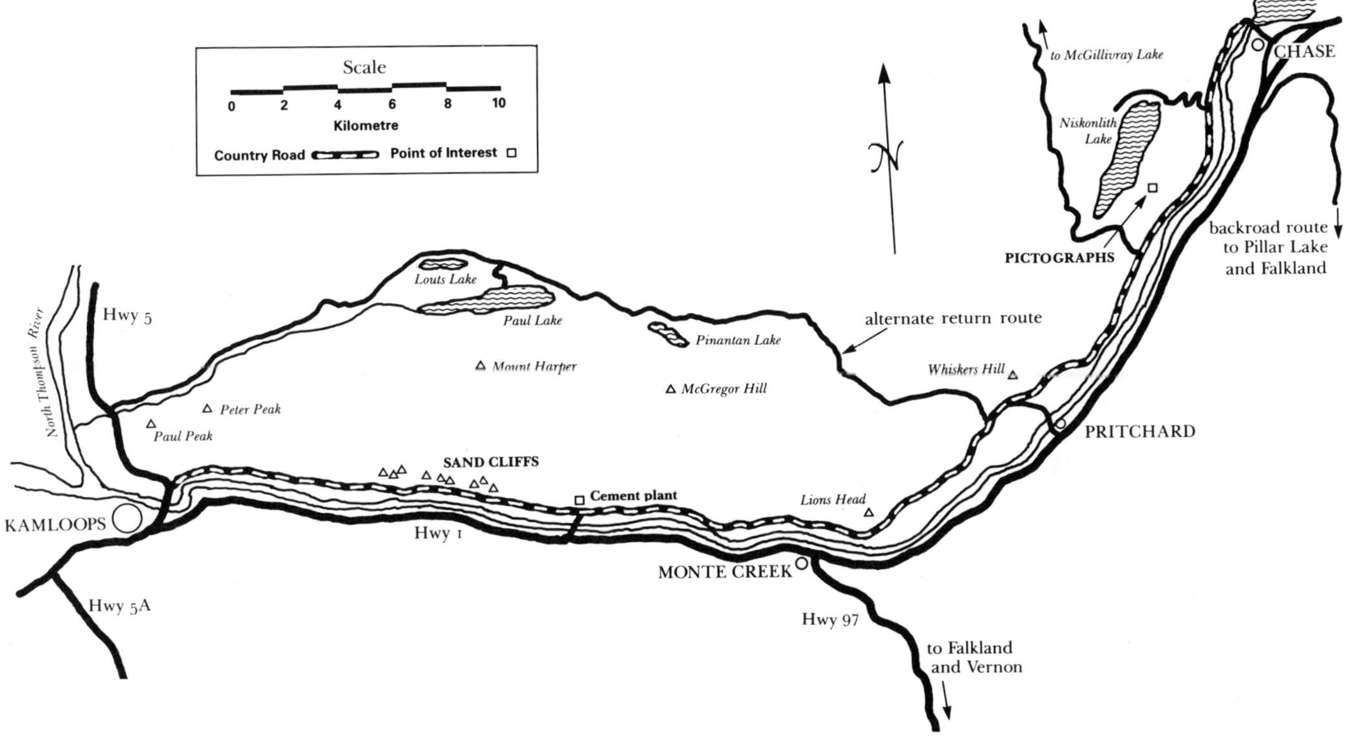

road narrows drastically as the river undercuts the shoreline then the valley broadens out again into green fields. Across the river, you can just make out the little settlement of Monte Creek—the antique shop in the old station flies a large Union Jack. This is the spot, formerly known as Ducks, where train-robber Bill Miner stopped and boarded a CPR train, his story popularized in the movie "The Grey Fox".

The rock bluff nearby is known as the Lion's Head because of its profile and here the Thompson River valley which has been following a course almost due east from Kamloops strikes a new direction to the northeast. At 30 kilometres the road leaves the river and cuts inland, climbing through a wooded gulley and out onto benchland above river level. The country here is still arid sagebrush scrub and pine, but watch carefully: within the next 20 kilometres two biotic zones will merge, the Interior Dry Belt with the Interior Wet Belt. The land will become greener and by the time you reach Chase all the sagebrush will be gone. A road signposted to Pinanton, Paul and Hyas Lake leads north at around 37 kilometres providing access to good fishing and a circle route back to Kamloops via Paul Lake provincial park.

Two kilometres farther a road sidles down a most inviting gap towards broad green fields and a narrow wooden bridge which crosses the river to the community of Pritchard (an escape route to Highway 1 if you need it.) Walter Pritchard, a driver for the Okanagan Stage Lines, settled here in 1912 and built a store and a hotel. Resist the temptation to go to Pritchard and keep on the Chase road which stays high above the river, cutting around the steep bluff of Whiskers Hill. There are nesting boxes for bluebirds on the fences here.

The forest road to McGillivray Lake angles north at around the 47 kilometre mark, providing access to a network of backroads which wind through the hills from Louis Creek to Adams Lake. Drive slowly now. When you cross a creek around a bend in the road by a ranch house and an old orchard, stop and scan the hillside above you. The granite bluffs on the skyline are painted with Indian pictographs and the site alone is well worth the thirty minute hike up through the trackless meadows, knee-deep in flowers in late spring. The red motifs are painted where overhanging boulders have created two small caves and water seeping between the cracks runs over the rocks to create a slippery cascade in wet weather. A careful search will reveal pictographs of eagles, deer, bearpaw tracks, human figures, crosses and a pattern of arrows carefully placed along the lines of quartz in the rock. It's a great place just to be, and the view is beautiful.

Back on the road, drive north, stopping to watch the action at an osprey's nest on top of a prominent power pole. A road to Niskonlith Lake with

Left: Eroded sandstone cliffs on the quiet side of the Thompson River.

Top: Indian pictographs on a hilltop near Niskonlith.

Below left: Among the sandstone hoodoos; right: Paul Lake provincial park.

Above: Ranch enfolded in the Alberta Foothills.

Right: The pioneer settlement of Maycroft.

Above: The long unyielding ridge of the Livingstone Range north of Burmis.

Left: The Gap in the Livingstones, cut through by the Oldman River.

Six kilometres past the bridge is the old Maycroft schoolhouse and a little farther on lies the community church; it has lost its steeple but still looks out at the world through mock-Gothic windows. Nearby, a big old square stone house, one of four similar heritage houses in the area, stands derelict behind a marshy pond. To the north the billowing green hills are easy on the eye. A sign announces the start of the Bow-Crow Forest Reserve and warns that the road is not maintained in winter.

It may have been near Maycroft that Fidler, ever curious, made arrangements to journey farther south to meet and trade with the Kootenay Indians who had never before seen a white man. With an Indian guide he journeyed farther up the Oldman and passed through the famous Gap, a geological tour de force, where the river has cut a dramatic S-shape gorge through the otherwise unbroken mountain barrier. East of the Gap, Fidler was shown the Old Man's Bowling Green, "a place where Indians formerly assembled to play at a particular game . . . by rolling a small hoop of 4 inches diameter and darting an arrow out of the hand after it". Apparently the object of the game was to throw the arrow through the centre of the rolling hoop. Fidler described the scene in his journal. The ball court was marked by stones "about the bigness of a person's fist above the ground . . . close set and neatly put together." In addition there were eleven piles of stones around the perimeter that Fidler thought may have been seats for umpires.

"On my enquiring concerning the origin of this spot, the Indians gave me a surprising and ridiculous account", continued Fidler. "They said that a white man . . . came from the south many years ago and built this for the Indians to play at . . . They also say that this same person made the buffalo on purpose for the Indians. They describe him as a very old, white-headed man and several more things very ridiculous." Fidler drew in his journal a plan of this strange ball court, the only picture there is of this fascinating and ancient site. Early geologists journeying through the Gap and oldtime ranchers were also familiar with it but before archaeologists could investigate, a combination of floods and roadbuilding destroyed all traces.

Fidler's journal places the Bowling Green 1.2 kilometres below the confluence of Racehorse Creek, along a north-south section of the river. This would put it at around 21 kilometres from the junction with Highway 22 at the river bridge. There are several flat benches in this area and plenty of boulders the size of a man's fist. But the exact location has been lost.

By now the road is into the evergreen forests of the foothills. Just beyond the "Bowling Green" flats is the junction with Road 940, the Forestry Trunk which is signposted south to Coleman (35 kilometres) and north all the way to the Trans Canada Highway (167 kilometres). Turn north and drive over the bridge across roaring Racehorse Creek. Fly Hill to the west is green and grassy, with a line of eroded rimrocks, and the area is thick with aspens. Two kilometres past the junction is Livingstone Gap Fire Base, and a little farther lies Gap Pond, a former highways department gravel pit which has been filled with water and stocked with cutthroat trout. Maintained by the forestry department this makes a fine break in the journey, particularly if you want fresh fish for supper.

A few kilometres farther north is Dutch Creek which flows down from Tornado Pass on the continental divide, near the impressive spires of Tornado Mountain and the high glaciated hump of Gould Dome. A rough road follows the river up into its headwaters, a good access route for mountain hikers. There is a forestry campsite near the creek crossing and a sign pointing out the Livingstone Fire Lookout just to the east, a high point at 2,160 metres. The Forestry Trunk Road stays to the west of the Oldman River, passing alternately through evergreens and clumps of aspens for another five kilometres then it crosses the river and enters the valley of its tributary, the Livingstone.

The Oldman rises high under the spine of the Rockies. A road follows the river upstream for 20 kilometres to Beehive Natural Area, more than 800 hectares of pristine old-growth spruce-fir forest set aside as a wildlife reserve for bears, elk, moose and bighorn sheep. Though the Upper Oldman valley retains its wilderness aspect, it has been well used by man ever since the first prehistoric Indians hunted in these high regions, built cairns to mark passes and cache sites and set up spring and fall camps. Europeans later mined the area for lead and zinc. The riverside road was originally built to provide access to the Galena Mine high on the slopes of Mount Gass and enthusiasts can still locate the old mine shafts and abandoned equipment, including an ore car. The road today is well travelled by hunters, anglers and hikers en route to the north-south Divide Trail, one of Alberta's premier hiking routes.

The Forestry Trunk Road forges north, with the Livingstone River as its guide. Contrary to expectations, the road is not totally hemmed in by trees; there are just enough stretches of broad

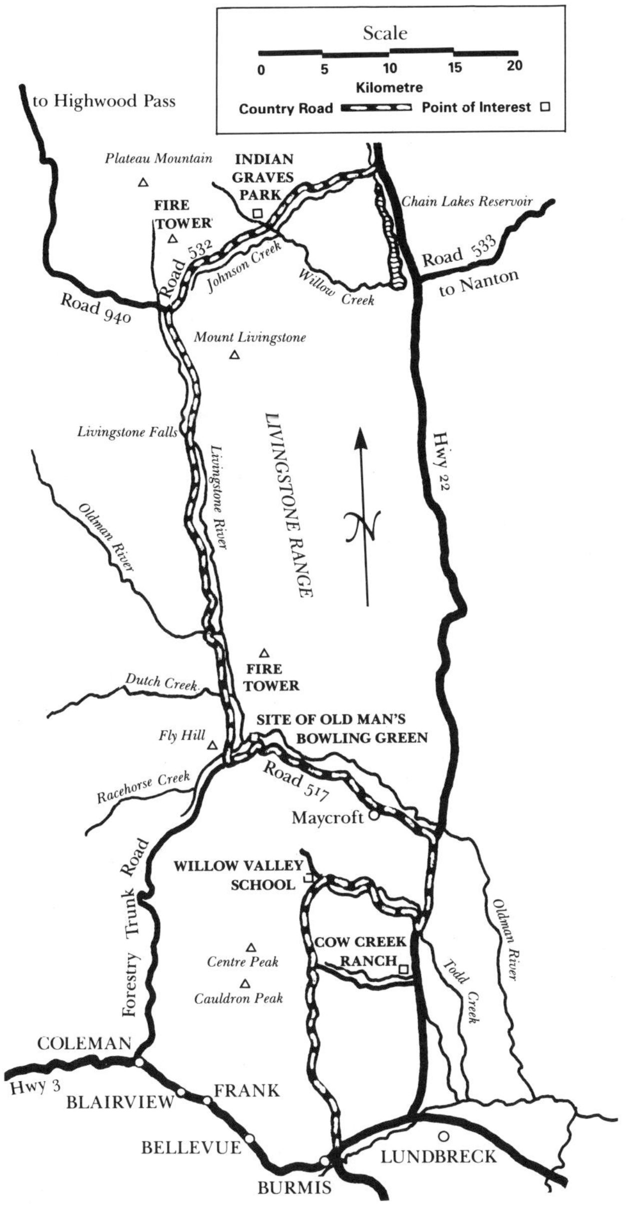

grassy valley and open meadows to prevent forest claustrophobia and to permit unhindered views of the mountains—Horseshoe Ridge of the Livingstones to the east, Cabin Ridge and Twin Peaks of the Front Range to the west. At Livingstone Falls the river splits into twin cascades. The falls are geologically unique: the rock ledges have been thrust upwards against the flow of the river and the water slides down the sloping rock instead of falling over. The forest shade and the bright chatter of the river make this a popular camping spot.

Northeast lies the peak of Mount Livingstone and ahead looms the huge high bare shoulder of Plateau Mountain, where the Livingstone River rises. This mountain massif is interesting because its broad treeless summit is covered with rocks apparently set in a sort of patchwork quilt design of polygonal and circular patterns. No, this is not another Indian ball court but a feature entirely natural, a relic of the Ice Age when the summit dome rose high above the Pleistocene ice, a rocky island surrounded by a glacial sea, subject to long spells of intense, cracking cold. Maps show several roads leading to the top of Plateau Mountain and a section has been set aside as a Natural Area.

About 60 kilometres from Highway 22 (or 112 kilometres from Burmis) the Forestry Trunk Road angles west to forge its way over into the Highwood River valley and Secondary Road 532 heads east, signposted to Nanton. Turn right (east) here. The road follows a narrow valley and climbs steadily. It is not recommended for vehicles towing trailers because of steep grades and sharp switchbacks. Without warning, it leaves the forests behind and emerges, breathless, into the sub-alpine, a windy region of raw rock slopes and lingering snow patches. In no more than four kilometres it reaches an 1,800 metre pass beside a perfectly circular icy alpine tarn confronted with a steep and spectacular drop-off into the Johnson Creek valley. Ahead, there's an endless view of green and forested hills, and then the haze of the prairies. The height and the view are unexpected, and breathtaking. Without obvious effort, the road has crossed over the spine of the Livingstone Range and now must make a far more precipitous descent. It's an exciting road, but it is also a lonely road. You needn't worry about meeting another vehicle around one of the hairpin bends, but you might have a long wait for help, if you run into trouble.

As you drive cautiously down the mountain zig-zags you can, in places, look back to see the thin line of the road snaking down from the skyline. But all too soon the road loses its wild alpine character and meanders gently through foothill rangeland, dappled with aspen and bright in June with masses of dandelions. Where Johnson Creek flows into the Willow, Indian Graves Recreation Area provides good camping. It's a popular trailhead for horse packtrips and there are corrals nearby. To the east of the corrals, a high rock ridge rises up like the fluted ribs and backbone of some prehistoric beast. Just over the creek crossing is the grave itself—a white wooden cross fenced off by pickets.

At little more than 20 kilometres from that high and desolate alpine summit, the road reaches civilization: the hurly-burly of traffic on Highway 22 just north of Chain Lakes reservoir. Here you have a choice: to head north to Longview, Turner Valley and Calgary, or south back to the Crowsnest Pass. Or you can connect with any one of a number of routes east across the Porcupine Hills.

FRASER VALLEY DAYTRIP

The largest area of fertile farmland in the whole of British Columbia, the Fraser Valley stretches less than 150 kilometres from the town of Hope, at its narrow neck, to the sprawling river delta on the Pacific. From earliest times, men found this an easy transportation route. Indians, fur-traders, the traffic of the goldrush, the first settler's trails, two transcontinental railways and a great highway all followed the valley down to the sea. And on the sea at the river's mouth, Canada's third largest metropolis sprawls ever larger. Each year more farmland is lost to suburbia.

Most Vancouverites experience the Fraser Valley at speed, dashing along the freeway route south of the river and bypassing all the valley settlements on their way east to the Interior. But if you've a mind for the slower pace of country roads,

Above: The frosted fields of an island winter

Opposite Page: A thrust of juicy spring dandelions by a Barnston Island barn.

the valley has much to offer. Look at any large scale map and you will see that the green fields are cross-hatched by a network of little meandering roads that lead to any destination you have in mind: from the U.S. border to the Fraser River's bridges; from the Vancouver suburbs all the way to Hope. It would take a lifetime of Sundays to explore them all. Many are best travelled on foot or by bicycle for speed tends to diminish the lovely details of the countryside: wildflowers in the ditches, a lacy line of trees, dew on spider's webs, the serenity of munching cows.

This country road, a favourite for a spring day's outing, takes you to Barnston Island, on to Fort Langley, then along the river to the daffodil fields of Bradner. And Bradner Road will bring you south all the way to the U.S. border where Boundary or Zero Road provides an interesting return route to Vancouver.

To reach Barnston Island, drive west on the Highway 1 freeway over the Port Mann bridge and take Exit 53 onto 176 Street, the road south to Cloverdale. Turn north, cross back over the freeway, noticing Anniedale heritage schoolhouse on display here, and head down the hill towards the river. When you meet 104 Avenue at the bottom of the hill, turn right (east) and drive to the ferry landing. Barnston is one of several little silty islands washed up by the Fraser and it's the only one served by public ferry. Operated for the Department of Highways to link the island residents with the mainland, the ferry is an odd combination of an open barge for vehicles and passengers and a jaunty tugboat which noses the barge across the river. The ferry is free and runs on demand, staying at the island dock in between runs. It's a busy route. On a sunny Sunday the ferry operates continuously and there is often a lineup of cars and biycles. If Sunday is your day for a drive, then start early.

Barnston is small, a fat triangle about three kilometres wide and two broad, and it lies so low in the water that it had to be dyked to prevent flooding. The paved narrow road on top of the dyke makes it possible to circle the island in a matter of minutes, if speed is your object. But the island needs time to be appreciated. Leave your car on the mainland and cross the river as a foot passenger or bring your bicycles as many families do. At any time of year a slow walking tour of Barnston will bring you close to the countryside.

The island's population centres along the southeastern shore. Many are fishermen; steps lead down from the gardens to tiny wharves where boats are moored and fishnets spread out to dry. But the rest of the island, safe within its sheltering dyke and threaded with drainage canals, is almost deserted. There are lush, untidy meadows dotted with black and white Frisian cows; there are old barns and milking sheds, horses and sheep and the simple barnyard things you thought you had forgotten: the cry of a bronzy cockerel, the territorial barking of farm dogs, a cat mousing in the hedges, the smell of manure. In winter, the dyke road is dry underfoot and provides a bracing walk with good views of the mountains across frosty island fields. In spring and summer, unpaved bushy lanes angling through the island's centre can also be explored. And there is good fishing from the sandbars at the island's northern tip.

Give yourself a good three hours to walk around the island, more if you stop to watch the birds or pick blackberries, then cross back to the mainland and retrace your way towards the freeway. Before you cross the freeway, however, turn left (east) onto 96 Avenue and follow this and Wilson Crescent into Fort Langley. Before the recent spread of Langley suburbs this road was pleasantly rural but today there are new subdivisions, industrial parks and shopping centres.

The village of Fort Langley nearly 12 kilometres from the freeway junction is one of the province's oldest settlements, dating back to 1839 when the Hudson's Bay Company built a post here. Today the fort is a national park; inside the stout stockade with its single lookout tower, gun slots and cannon, the atmosphere of the mid 19th century has been well captured, though only one of the buildings, the white-washed store, is original. In summer months, park personnel don traditional clothes and go to work: making barrels in the cooperage, swapping yarns and showing off the furs behind the store counter, sawing wood, manning the forge in the blacksmith's shop, spinning and weaving and generally giving visitors entertainment as well as education for their money. The "Big House", beautifully reproduced in cedar, is furnished in period style, complete with some of the original pieces. The whole place is well worth seeing, and children love it.

The fort is clearly signposted from Glover Road, the village main street, and there are other things to see in the village, including many pioneer houses, a surprisingly large and dignified city hall, now the community centre, and a huge Victorian graveyard. The local tourist office has a pamphlet describing several walking tours of historic houses in the area.

The present fort is not the first that was built here. In 1827, facing increasingly urgent claims of American sovereignty over all the land then known as Oregon Country, the Hudson's Bay Company sent the schooner Cadboro up the Fraser to establish a trading post here, its first on the Pacific north of the Columbia River. Politically, this small outpost of empire was a very strong anchor for British territorial claims. And before the establishment of Fort Victoria in 1843, Fort Langley was the main coastal depot, the nucleus of future trade, industry and settlement. After twelve years of collecting and packaging furs and salting barrels of salmon the old fort was declared dilapidated and inconvenient. Under a new factor, James Yale, the men built a new and larger fort on higher ground closer to the fort farmland. The original buildings were abandoned. The site is important to the history of British Columbia but it is vacant now and unacknowledged, except by a solitary stone marker in an overgrown field. If you want to make a pilgrimage there, return down Wilson Crescent and make a right turn down Allard Crescent. The road

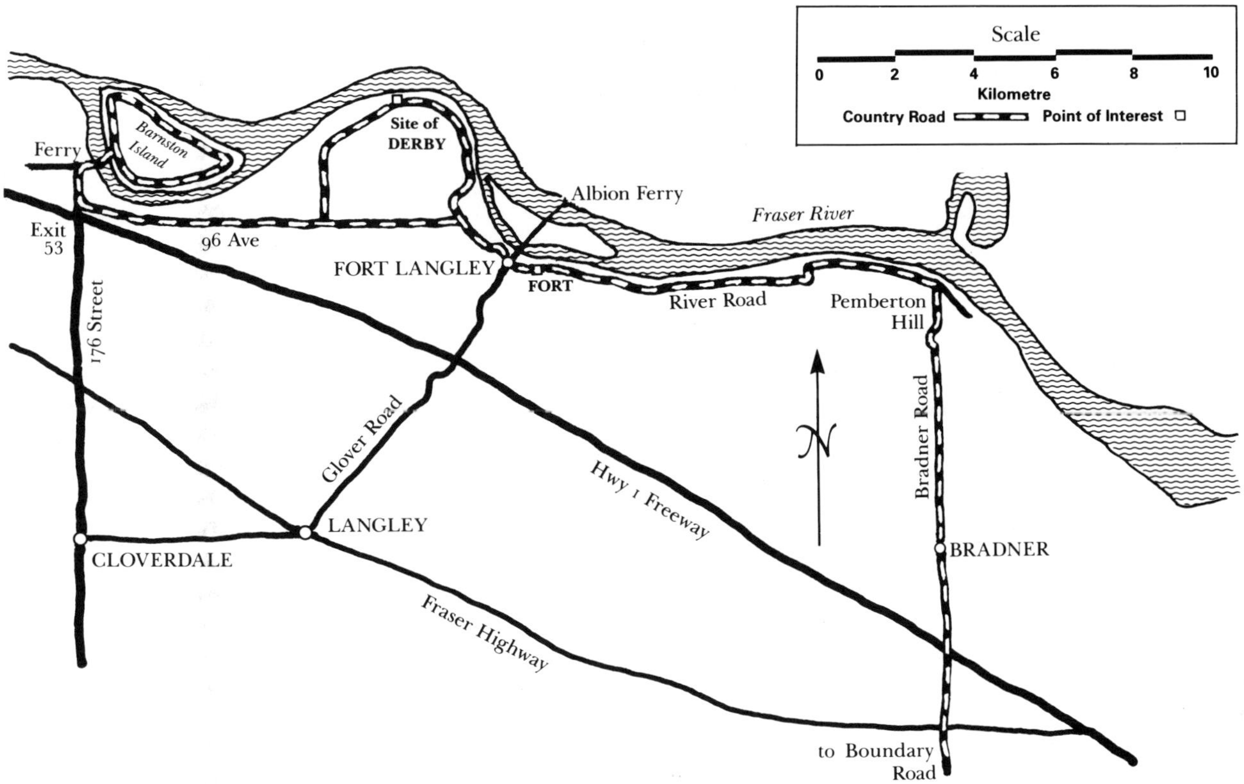

leads around the curve of the river to Derby Reach Regional Park on a river bar, a good place for camping and fishing. Here in a field overlooking the river, just about opposite an old house with a long front porch, is the site of the original fort, the birthplace of the province.

B.C.'s earliest governor, James Douglas, (for a while he also had the job of HBC Chief Factor) understood the significance of the first fort site. In 1858 he chose it for the location of a town, the prospective capital of the new Mainland Colony. Known as Derby after Britain's Prime Minister, the townsite was surveyed and lots went on sale in Victoria. Tenders were called for construction of a courthouse and jail, a church and a parsonage. The Royal Engineers were sent in to establish headquarters and build a barracks here, but when their chief Colonel Moody arrived, he was appalled. Not only was the townsite on the wrong side of the river for defensive purposes (they were always preparing against American attack) but the river here was not deep enough for sea-going ships. On top of that, the site was constantly under the threat of Fraser floodwater. A new townsite farther downstream on the north side of the river was chosen, and this became New Westminster. But by then, in Derby the church of St. John the Divine had been built, the parson was ensconced in his parsonage and the first service was held on May 1, 1859. Seven months later, the whole townsite, including the church, was abandoned. (The church, B.C.'s oldest, was moved in 1881 across the river to Maple Ridge where it stands today.)

Return to new Fort Langley and take River Road which follows the river under the fort's lone bastion. For a while, the embankment of the CN Railway obscures the river view but it's generally a pleasantly rural drive with the twin peaks of Golden Ears prominent to the north across McMillan Island with its white Indian church. Glen Valley an old settlement once served by river steamers, lies about eight kilometres from the fort at a road junction. Turn left here and keep going, right beside the river, for another three kilometres, then turn south and follow Bradner Road across the meadows and up the steep escarpment of Pemberton Hill Road. In wet or icy weather this steep section is sometimes closed to traffic. If this is the case, Le Feuvre Road to the west also leads to Bradner, though somewhat circuitously.

The Bradner area on its high and forested plateau was far from river access and was settled comparatively late, in 1895. The first farmer was Thomas Bradner but it was a later settler, Fenwick Fatkin who discovered that the soil and the climate here were very good for flowers. He started a bulb farm; others followed and today in mid-April there are fields of daffodils in bloom. At the peak of the

Barnston Island dykes provide dry footing for frosty winter walks.

Opposite Page, Top: Painted with fresh snow, the twin peaks of Golden Ears rise above green Fraser Valley fields. Bottom: The island ferry is free and comes on call, shares the river with logbooms and barges.

seaspan
439

season, thousands of the flowers are cut while in bud and shipped to markets across the country. Nearly every corner along Bradner Road has flower stands where you can buy bunches of field-fresh flowers often very cheaply.

While most of the growers are in the cut flower business and produce only the most popular varieties of daffodils, there are others who specialize in bulbs of exotic species for home gardeners. A good place to see these is at the Bradner Flower Show held at the community hall around Easter. Here you will discover that there are hundreds of different kinds of daffodils, from miniature to giant, single to double, from those with long trumpets to those with no trumpet at all, and in shades from white and all grades of yellow and orange to pink. If you like what you see, orders can be placed with the grower and the bulbs will be delivered in time for fall planting. The three-day flower show is a popular affair, bringing busloads of day trippers out from Vancouver. Country teas are served.

Continue south down Bradner Road, a rolling road which ducks under the freeway and continues on across Fraser Highway, becoming narrower and unpaved as it negotiates a hill around large gravel pits and a U-catch trout farm. Mostly though, the road is easy driving and refreshingly rural as it plummets straight south through raspberry fields to Huntingdon Road, where it jogs left before continuing on to meet Boundary Road for the return journey to Vancouver.

ON THE MURDER TRAIL

Some roads cover not so much distance as time, leading back into the past to events that colour our history and affect the way we look at the landscape. This country road south of Kamloops rambles through rolling ranchland well worth visiting for its own serene sake. But murder took place in these hills a hundred or so years ago and malevolence endures, darkening even the brightest colours of spring.

The story of these events reads like a traditional saga from the wild and woolly west: horse theft, jail break, chase by mounted posse, gunfire, death, a log-cabin siege, a swinging gallows. It's a well worn scenario, often played out in Hollywood. But this happened here. And you can visit the scene.

It is December, 1879, the weather well below zero with deep snow shrouding the hills and weighing down the branches of the pines. The heroes of the affair are John Tannatt Ussher, constable and government agent at Kamloops; William Palmer and John McLeod, ranchers, and Amni Shumway, a Mormon freighter. The villains are half-breed brothers Allan, Charlie and Archie McLean and their friend Alex Hare—hell-raisers, cattle-rustlers, thieves, jail-breakers, murderers.

The plot: The McLeans and Hare, imprisoned in Kamloops jail for stealing horses, escape and take to the hills. Back at his ranch, William Palmer misses his best stallion and goes riding up on Long Lake range to look for him. He finds the McLeans with his horse but he does not dare to confront them alone: he rides back to town to find Constable Ussher.

A posse is organized. Ussher swears in Palmer as special constable and persuades ace tracker Shumway, a pacifist who will never carry a gun, to lead them. It is early afternoon on Sunday, December 7; there is little more than two hours of daylight left when the men start off across the snowy hills to where the McLeans were last seen. Near Anderson Creek, Shumway picks up the fugitives' tracks leading south over the range. Following them in the fading light, they stop at the cabin of John McLeod and persuade him to join the posse. McLeod, an ex-policeman from Glasgow, is a good choice. When darkness falls, the four men spend the night at the camp of William Roxborough, who is wintering the horses and mules used by the CPR survey crews. Roxborough, too, decides to join them.

It is bitterly cold when the posse starts out early the next morning. The hills are bleak, obscured by falling snow. Southwards they go, following the faint tracks towards the hump of Brigade Hill. Roxborough spots some stray mules and, ever mindful of his job and the good of the CPR, he leaves the posse to chase them. It's now eleven o'clock. Hazily through the snowflakes, on an open flat circled by aspen trees, the men spot their quarry and move quietly in. The McLeans and Hare see them coming and raise their rifles. They seem to recognize Palmer and shoot at him, but they miss and the bullet grazes McLeod in the cheek. McLeod shoots back. His borrowed shotgun misfires and he takes another bullet, this time in the knee; his horse is also shot.

Constable Ussher takes a different approach. Knowing the boys are young and headstrong (the two youngest are barely in their teens) he leaves his gun in the saddle and walks towards them with open hands, pleading with them to throw down their guns and surrender. It is a mistake. He grabs Hare. Hare stabs him. Ussher reels. Then Archie McLean puts a gun to the constable's head and fires. Ussher lies crumpled and still on the bloodstained snow.

The other lawmen, one injured, one a pacifist

Opposite Page: The Ussher Monument, idyllic setting for the scene of a crime.

Left and Bottom: Barns on Rose Hill. Below: Brigade Lake, end of Day One from Kamloops on the HBC Trail.

and one with a cap-and-ball pistol so antiquated it is useless, retreat in shock, confer briefly and decide to ride back to Kamloops for reinforcements. The outlaws, swigging whisky for courage and to fend off the cold, strip the dead man of his clothes which they take for themselves, along with his horse and his gun, still strapped to the saddle. They ride south through the snow to a second senseless killing, a lonely old shepherd outside his cabin door.

This script has other colourful scenes to follow—of manhunt, siege and justice—and the tale ends with one of B.C.'s longest criminal trials and, sadly, a multiple hanging in New Westminster jail. If you want the full story read "We've Killed Johnny Ussher", a historical narrative very well told by Mel Rothenburger, himself a descendent of Donald McLean, a former factor of the Hudson's Bay fort at Kamloops and father of the "wild McLean boys".

Amazingly, in more than 100 years, much of the country where this all took place has seen little change and it is easy to retrace the trail and relive the events that happened here. It is mostly rangeland still, high and bleakly beautiful, up above the summer heat of the Thompson River valley and lying just to the west of Highway 5A, the old Merritt Road. The site of the Ussher murder itself, now marked by a stone cairn, provides a focal point for a journey of exploration through the hills—and back into time.

From a botanist's point of view, the hills hold attraction in themselves for a good year brings wildflowers in abundance, from the first shiny spring buttercups through to violets and yellow fritillaries, lupines and gaillardias. In fall, the aspens scattered in sparse clumps and running like rivulets in the gulleys of the hills, turn a clear bright gold. It is a country for larks and hawks, bluebirds and bobolinks, with lakes well stocked with waterbirds. History lovers will take an extra pleasure in knowing they follow a part of the fur brigade trail used by the Hudson's Bay Company in the years before 1848 to go from Fort Kamloops across to the Okanagan Valley. Brigade Lake (known as Long Lake to the pioneers and still marked as such on many maps) was the brigade campsite the first night out from the fort.

The Murder Trail begins at Knutsford, just south of Kamloops on Highway 5A. Here, by the community hall and ranks of mail boxes, Long Lake Road veers southwest. The fur brigades came up from Kamloops via Peterson Creek which the road, twisting and dipping, soon crosses. Roads lead off west to Goose Lake and Edith Lake but the brigade route continues south through ranch country, bordered by wild roses, geraniums, larkspur and lupines in early summer, and crosses Anderson Creek where the lawmen of old first came upon the McLean boys' tracks. About nine kilometres from Knutsford the large blue lake, seen only in glimpses through the trees on the west side of the road, is McLeod Lake, named for one of the protagonists in the saga. The low hill opposite commemorates the tracker, Shumway. At 14 kilometres, Jackson Road takes off eastward, the route to the murder site, but first, make a detour along the Brigade Trail which continues straight on, to the end of Day One on the fur traders' journey from Kamloops.

The huge brigades of the Hudson's Bay Company often included more than 300 packhorses, each loaded with 40 kg bales of furs, along with a retinue of 20 or so men and their horses. The chief trader might be leading them, dignified in his best fur hat, and sometimes the bagpipes would be skirling as they plodded along. Campsites for such large numbers of men and beasts were difficult to find: they had to have good grazing, lots of water and room for comfort. Brigade or Long Lake was perfect. It lies, a sinuous ripple of blue in the folds of the hills, about three kilometres from the junction, its ample grass surrounds now fenced as ranchers' fields. For all practical purposes the road dead ends at the end of the lake but birdwatchers will want to stay awhile; in spring and early summer when the ducks are nesting and in fall when migrants plop thankfully down it's a lake well worth study. An old deserted homestead across the lake invites dalliance and it is possible to explore this on foot by means of a grassy track which angles in from the Knutsford end of the lake.

But back to the Murder Trail. Retrace your way to the junction, take Jackson Road east for .7 kilometre, then drive south along Mannings Road for .6 kilometre to a gate by a series of corrals. Park your car here, walk through the gate and follow a track roughly southeast under a set of powerlines. In a couple of minutes you will be at the site where Constable John Ussher met his death. A circular clearing in the aspens beside a small unnamed pond (in dry years this may not be more than a mud puddle) is marked by a stark pyramid of granite inscribed to the memory of the Kamloops lawman "unarmed and fearless . . . who gave his life to secure peace and order in our growing West." In spring, wildflowers bloom in memoriam—mission bells, shooting stars, pink avens and violets—but the mood in the dappled gentle greens of the glade is, for those with imagination, melancholy.

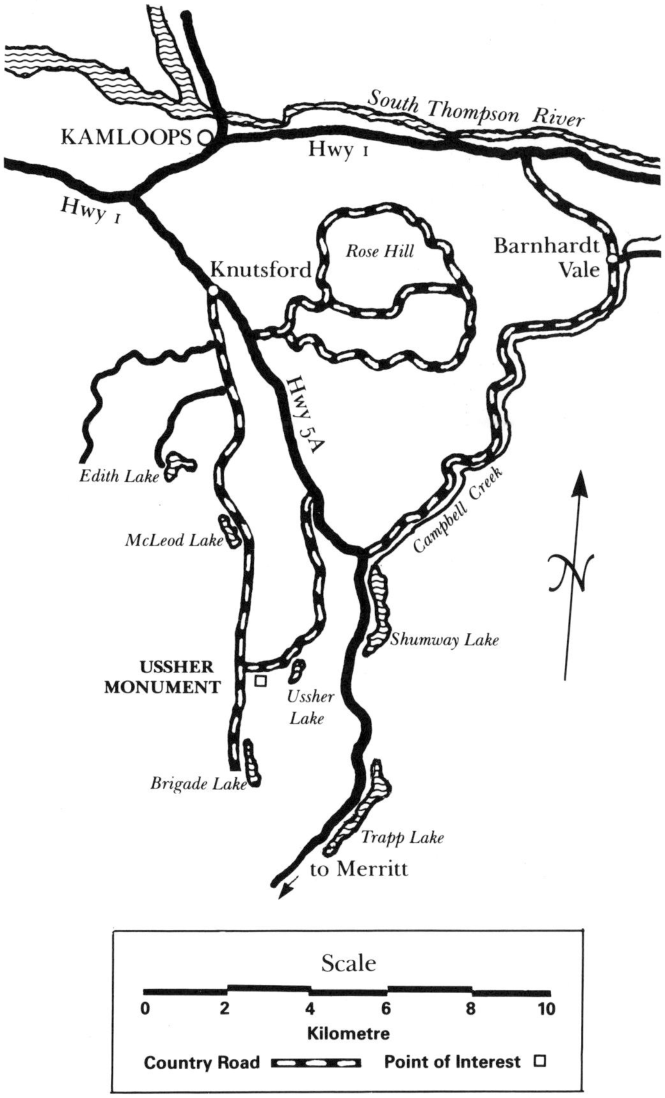

The murder scene is easily enacted. It must have been right here on that bitter December day that the McLean boys had their campsite. The posse crept up behind those trees. A horse whinnied, its breath steaming in the cold; guns were brandished; voices rang out. Maybe the shots startled a crow out of the aspens. Shumway, unarmed and terrified, crouched behind that slope and here, right beside the cairn, Ussher's blood flowered crimson in the snow.

After the shooting, the fugitives rode south along the Brigade Trail which met today's highway near Napier Lake, continued on to Stump Lake where they murdered shepherd James Kelly and finished up in a cabin at Douglas Lake where they were eventually captured. There are no country roads that follow the rest of the murderers' route but there is a pleasant alternative. Return to Jackson Road and follow it northeast past Ussher Lake and round the eastern slopes of Shumway Hill—all marvellous high rangeland—for a further 8.3 kilometres until it meets up with Highway 5A. The way is narrow, sinuous and sometimes dusty, but the beauty of the countryside is something to be remembered.

If you want more adventuring when you reach the highway, head south for nearly five kilometres. Just before Shumway Lake, where Amni Shumway homesteaded to winter his pack animals, a road heads northeast up Campbell Creek. It was to this valley that John McLeod, recovered from his wounds, moved in 1881. A bunkhouse built across the creek from the main family house still stands beside the road, its boards weathered to a deep and lovely brown. The road eventually links up with Barnhartvale Road; turn west along this to return to Kamloops via Highway One.

Another option is Rose Hill, a little more than eight kilometres north on the highway. This loosely knit community was first settled in the early 1900s when families came up from Kamloops to carve small homesteads on the high grassland. Today, most of the smallholdings have been swallowed up by larger ranches but the land is the same, high and heady. Take Rosehill Road off the highway, then diverge onto Old Rosehill Road which circles the area. It is glorious rolling countryside, much of it unfenced, rich in old barns and homesteads, little lakes, hayfields, meadowlarks, soaring hawks and perching kestrels.

Rose Hill holds pleasant memories. One unforgettable fall morning as we dawdled along the lanes we disturbed a field of Canada geese bedded down for the night and now breakfasting in the hay. They rose with strident voices and a clamour of wings, circled darkly in the sky, then strung out in honking chains headed for the south. All that morning we watched the convoys in the sky, flying over Rose Hill as if this was a landmark on their flight path. And one spring, when patches of snow still stained the fields, our visit coincided with a migration of rough-legged hawks. There were dozens of them, perching sleepily on posts within arm distance. Rose Hill is a lovely area indeed, quite as lovely as its name. And as far away from thoughts of murder as one could wish to be.

EXPLORING THE COWICHAN VALLEY

The Indians called the Cowichan area "The Warm Land" perhaps because of temperature but more likely for its welcoming aspect and the ease of life here, in the sheltered bay with the forests and mountains at its back. The white settlers noticed the huge sweeps of arable land—at a premium on mountainous Vancouver Island. As early as 1862, the HMS Hecate sailed into the bay from Victoria and off-loaded a hundred would-be farmers, the second agricultural settlement on the island. For the farmers the land was free: the government paid off the local Indians to the tune of two blankets per head.

Settled and cleared early, the Cowichan Valley today has a neat and nurtured look, a tempting counterbalance to the rugged forests that lie all about and on which the whole economy of the island and the province was established. This country road enjoys the best of both worlds—the rich meadows and marshes at the head of Cowichan Bay and the deep forests that enshroud the lake.

The city of Duncan makes a convenient base of operations. It is touted as the City of the Totems because of the nearly 60 native totems which embellish the streetscape, all of them by local carvers. Also here is the Native Heritage Centre, its big house built like a traditional cedar plank longhouse where you can watch native carvers and other craftsmen at work, enjoy Indian storytelling and other entertainment and sample the local cuisine. Interestingly, the best known artifact from the Duncan area is the raw wool Fair-Isle pattern Cowichan sweater. The first settlers taught the Indians to knit, using wool from local sheep and traditional patterns from the Scottish islands. Today, their Fair-Isle designs complemented by Indian motifs, these hand-knitted sweaters are in demand. Just north of the city is the B.C. Forest Museum with an operating narrow gauge steam train and working machinery and artifacts from all facets of the pioneer logging industry.

From Duncan take the Trans Canada Highway south across the Koksilah River bridge and continue south past Whippletree Junction, a quaint little shopping mall with heritage buildings, many from Duncan's old Chinatown, that have been rescued, restored and relocated. Turn left just before the firehall on Koksilah Road and left again on Cowichan Bay Road. This leads through the community of the same name, worth a stop, particularly if you're interested in wooden boats (check out the Maritime Centre) and continues around the head of the bay where the two rivers, Koksilah and Cowichan, plus a maze of other smaller streams, sloughs, backwaters and old channels keep the meadows lush and green.

It is peaceful and pastoral, much the way that poet Robert Service of Yukon fame must have seen

Top: Mist on Cowichan Lake at Gordon Bay.

Centre left: Skutz Falls fish ladders on the Cowichan River.

Centre Right: On the boardwalk at Bamfield. Cars stop on the opposite shore.

Opposite Page: Yellow violets in the Honeymoon Bay wildflower reserve.

Right: The third church of St. Ann at Cowichan Bay, from the rectory garden.

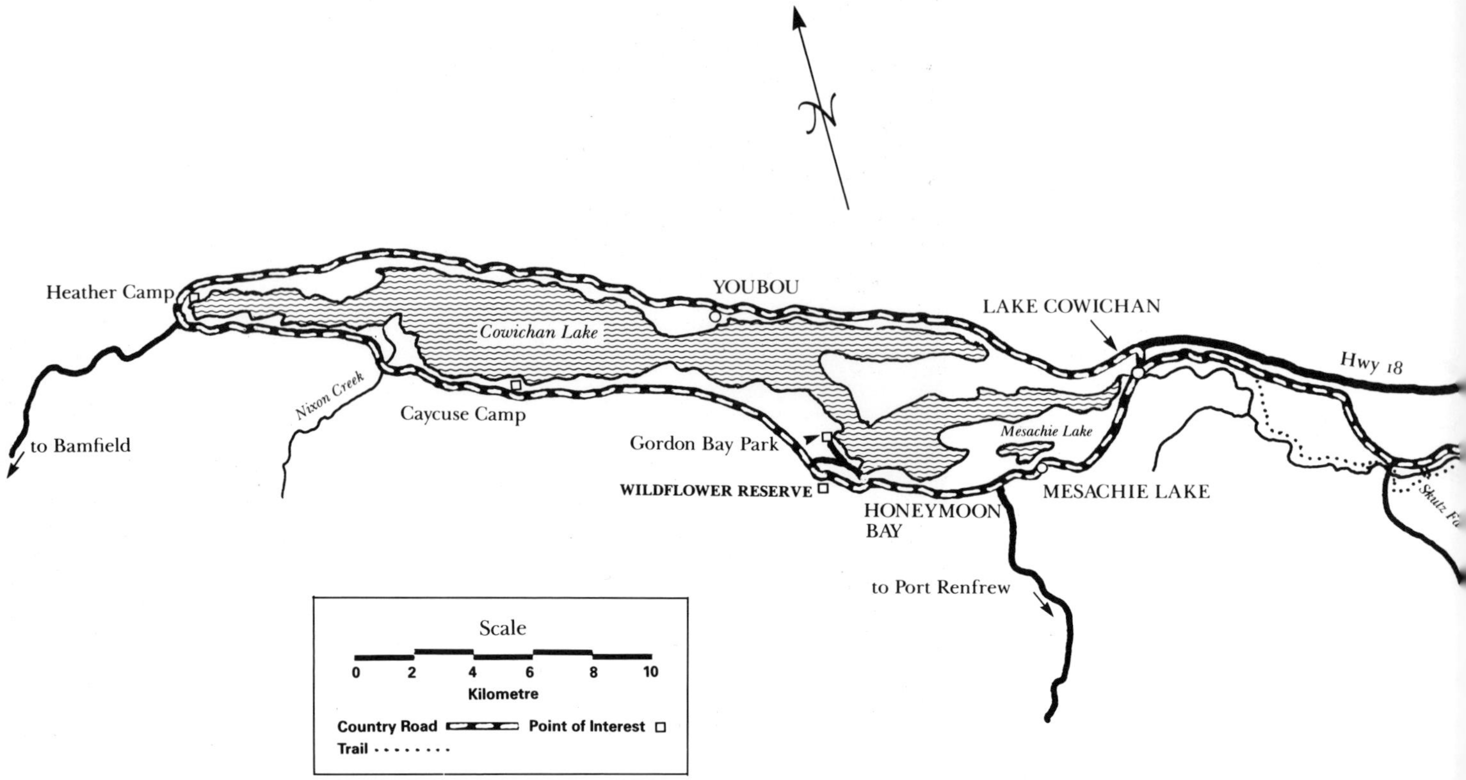

it when he came out from England to work in the valley in 1894. After a stint in California, Service returned in 1901 to work at the Corfield store and post office and to tutor the seven Corfield boys. He left for Victoria four years later to become a bank clerk and he was transferred to the Yukon the following year. Close to the site of the store where Service worked, a small stone cairn commemorates the arrival of the hundred pioneer farmers.

Today much of the land around the mouth of the Cowichan River is Indian Reserve. The road crosses the railway leading out to the deep sea dock in the middle of the bay, then the main channel of the river. Straight ahead, beautifully silhouetted against the sky on the top of Comiaken Hill lies the stark outline of the old stone church of St. Ann. In ruins now and lacking its little domed belfry, the church has also lost its solitary splendour as the Indian village edges nearer. But it is still worth a visit. Park below the bluff and walk up the rock-lined ramp and try not to let the unkempt air of the place ruin your appreciation for the fine stonework, elegant proportions and simple gothic windows.

This abandoned church, built by Father Pierre Rondeault in 1869 to replace an earlier log structure, has a remarkable history. The stone for its construction was quarried from the site by local Indians who broke up the stone with an old cannon ball fired into the village long before from HMS Thetis. The fine-grained sandstone was then shaped by expert stonemason William Williams from Victoria who charged a flat fee of $500. This was paid by the priest who raised the money by selling butter from his farm. The church was known thereafter as the Butter Church.

Services were held here until 1880 when the stone church was replaced by a larger one made of wood, located nearer to the Indian residential school just outside the reserve. The stone church, its doors and windows removed and distributed throughout the diocese, gradually fell into disrepair. It was later partly restored but today lies again a gaunt and empty shell. A little way down the road the "new" St. Ann's is a pleasing white frame building with a tall steeple, set on the hillside above a large and tousled graveyard. This church dates from 1890: the first replacement was destroyed by fire.

Cowichan Bay Road by this time has turned into Tzouhalem Road and turns west, heading back to Duncan. Indian Road leads north to a park at the tip of Quamichan Lake. The next intersection is Lakes Road. Turn north here and head

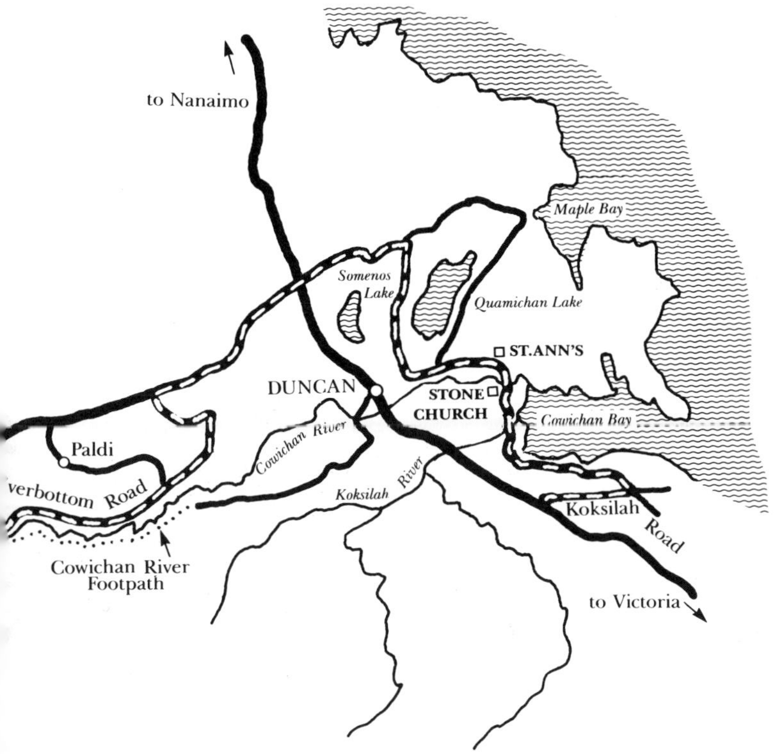

through the countryside between Quamichan and Somenos Lakes to a junction with Herd Road. Turn left (west) here, head back to the Trans-Canada and take Highway 18 to Lake Cowichan. (To avoid confusion, remember that the lake is Cowichan Lake; the name of the village on the lake is Lake Cowichan.)

Highway 18 is a new road, wide and straight but watch for a turning signed to Sahtlam Lodge on your left (south). Exit here and head down to the Cowichan River, a stream famous among anglers for feisty brown trout in summer and huge winter steelhead. When you reach Riverbottom Road, turn right (west). As its name suggests, this road follows the river for most of the 25 kilometres to Lake Cowichan, a delightful country road with easy access to the river at several places. Where the valley pinches in at Marie Canyon the road is forced onto the steep hillside. Here the forest service has provided a small but delicious recreation site, perched on the lip of the canyon with a steep stairway down to the river. In spring, the flowers here are beautiful.

At Skutz Falls, farther west, concrete fish ladders were built in 1955 to help migrating salmon upstream. There are two forestry campsites here. The second (most westerly) provides direct access to the fish ladders and the rock slabs of the exposed river bed. A highlight of a riverside picnic by the falls used to be the narrow and swaying pedestrian suspension bridge threaded high above the foaming water but this, alas, has been replaced by a road bridge for logging truck access. Over this bridge, the Cowichan River Trail, a footpath engineered originally for fishermen, crosses over from the south side to the north. The trail runs for 30 kilometres beside the river from just outside Duncan to Lake Cowichan, a hefty hike if taken in one gulp. The bridge is just about at the half-way point.

Beyond Skutz Falls, Riverbottom Road turns away from the river and angles back to rejoin Highway 18. But just before the junction, take Old Cowichan Lake Road instead, a narrow, slower and far prettier route that leads right into the village. The community was founded on lumber. Cowichan Lake, the largest on Vancouver Island, provided an easy means of transport for the rich haul of timber cut from surrounding river valleys. At one time there were three large sawmills in operation and two railways to haul the wood to market. Today, only one mill survives and both railways have abandoned tracks. The CN's trestle bridge across the river mouth has been kept intact as a convenient footbridge to Riverside Park.

From the village centre, drive past the museum in Kaatza Station and continue around the lake in a clockwise direction, heading towards Mesachie Lake, a small community which became even smaller when its sawmill closed in 1986. Here a logging mainline road takes off south to Port Renfrew on the West Coast, about 40 kilometres of rough travel with logging trucks for company. Drive with headlights on—and be prepared to pull over. Logging traffic has right of way.

Honeymoon Bay about 12 kilometres farther along used to be an industrial smudge on the lake with log booms crowding the water and smoke from the mill obscuring the view. The sawmill closed down: bad news for the economy but good news in terms of scenery. The place today is neat and tidy with a golf course, cottages, resorts and a large provincial park campground on the lake at Gordon Bay. A trail from the end of the beach here follows an old road up to an abandoned copper mine. Honeymoon Bay was first settled in 1886 by Henry March who took his produce to market at Duncan in a three-day trek by raft and ox-team. It was named (in anticipation) when another bachelor settler took off back east to fetch a bride and never returned.

Just beyond Honeymoon Bay, the wildflower reserve beside Sutton Creek provides a chance to

Left and Opposite Page, top: Trilliums and erythroniums brighten Vancouver Island woods in April.

Below Left: The Old Stone Church of St. Ann at Cowichan Bay near Duncan stands derelict on Comiaken Hill.

Below Right: Moss-wrapped maples in Caycuse Campsite, one of the loveliest on Cowichan Lake.

explore the forest on foot. The network of interconnecting trails leads down beside the creek under a green canopy of evergreens and alder, draped with ragged banners of moss. In April, the ferny floor is bright with wildflowers—including the rare and protected trillium and the even rarer pink erythronium.

Driving hour after hour along roads hemmed in by trees, the horizon obscured, can sometimes be claustrophobic. But walking slowly along these padded spongy trails and taking time to examine the small delights of nature—the spiral unfolding of a fern, the patterns of twigs and leaves, the textures of moss and the trail of a snail—gives one a new appreciation of the rainforest. These are not virgin stands of timber. The forests here, growing quickly on the rich soil of the protected slopes and easy to reach, have been harvested more than once and were allowed to regenerate naturally. From a forester's point of view the resulting mixture of evergreens and deciduous trees and shrubs is not desirable in terms of yield but to a layman's eye it is beautiful.

The pavement ends at Honeymoon Bay and for most of the way around the lake the road is gravel, dusty at times, particularly when a loaded logging truck blazes through. A new section of road climbs above the lake for a good vista often made romantically blue and misty by the steam from the mill at Youbou on the opposite shore. The lake is still used for transport: there is often a tugboat hauling a logboom in the picture, too.

If you have time to stop at only one lakeside campsite, then Caycuse is probably the most beautiful. Here the forest is almost entirely deciduous, mostly big-leaf maple, and the trunks are smothered in great bumpy bandages of soft green moss. Emblazoned in fall with soft russet colours, the site is also beautiful in early spring before the leaves cover up the sky. A short loop nature trail leads through the woods, crossing a little dry creek on a rustic hump-back bridge.

The Fletcher Challenge Caycuse works yard five kilometres farther west marks the location of one of the first seed orchards in B.C. beside Nixon Creek. Here prime trees are allowed to grow unchecked and their yearly crop of seeds is collected to supply tree nurseries.

Beyond Caycuse, the road becomes twisty and narrow, riding for several long stretches very close to the lake's edge. At the narrow western tip of the lake is a major road intersection: a left (south) turn here will take you over a low divide and into the valley of the Nitinat River, south to the shore of Nitinat Lake and west to Franklin Camp for connections to Bamfield and the West Coast Trail, or Port Alberni. Nitinat Lake, protected at its southern end by Pacific Rim National Park, is a long, thin lake (geologically an inlet) connected to the ocean at Whyac and racked by daily tides and blustery winds. The water is strongly salt and the rocky shoreline at low tide is embroidered with sea anemones and starfish. Nitinat and the nearby lakes of the Nitinat Triangle provide some of the finest wilderness canoeing in B.C.—and fierce windsurfing. The Nitinat Mainline also gives access to the Carmanah Valley and its trails through the big trees of this unlogged watershed which environmentalists want to preserve. There are clear signposts to follow here.

Hikers walking the West Coast Trail may want to drive to Bamfield, the village at its northernmost end. This will take a good couple of hours from the head of Cowichan Lake along well-surfaced logging roads that are open for public use at all times. Bamfield is worth a visit, even if you don't plan on a long hike. The village is in two halves: the road reaches the eastern half but the older more interesting section lies across the inlet, a pretty straggle of cottages along the shore connected by boardwalk and country trail and punctuated by seemingly dozens of docks. Until the road was punched through several years ago boats were Bamfield's lifeline to the outside world and this maritime heritage has been kept alive. The chief supply route is still the Lady Rose, a packet freighter built in Scotland in 1937 that carries mail, cargo and passengers down from Port Alberni three times a week. If you want to shed the shackles of auto dependency for a while, a stay at Bamfield can be thoroughly recommended.

Our country road, however, is not ambitious enough to venture all the way to the West Coast. Instead, from the head of Cowichan Lake it keeps going north for a while past another idyllic lakeside campsite (this one is called Heather) then swings around to complete the circle tour on the north side of the lake. Past Shaw Creek's meadow delta where summer brings sweet wild strawberries and across the rushing creeks of McKay and Wardroper the road leads past two more campsites before turning to pavement at the sawmill community of Youbou. Named for pioneer lumbermen Young and Blount, Youbou brings you back to civilization and it is only another 23 kilometres of smooth, dust-free driving back to Lake Cowichan and the highway back to Duncan.

THE OLDEST CARIBOO TRAIL

Of all the country roads in southern British Columbia, the old goldrush trail along the Upper Fraser River is the longest by far, 230 meandering kilometres from Pavilion in the south to Williams Lake. Along this road the human touches are few and kindly; the settlements old, the scenery incredible. It is a slow road, a dusty road, a lonely road, one of the very best introductions to the romantic vision of landscape and history known as the Cariboo.

The route follows the River Trail of 1859 which begins north of Lillooet at Pavilion, one of the oldest settlements in the Interior. Here beside Highway 12 the old general store, in summer a blaze of garden flowers, provides a last chance to stock up on supplies. Pavilion is a corruption of the French word "pavillon" or flag and was so named after the Indian graveyard marked with white flags that early French Canadian travellers saw here. Pavilion is perched high above the Fraser River's narrow and precipitous upper canyon. The B.C. Railway threads its way along the canyon sides on its way to Clinton and points north, but the old trail (and later the first leg of the wagon road) kept high above the river, seeking easier terrain. On it goes, winding up the mountain, to the old 22-Mile House at the Indian village north of the store. Lillooet was the original Mile Zero of the Cariboo Road which went this way for only two years, from 1861 to 1863 when it was replaced by a road up the Fraser and Thompson rivers from Yale. Wagon road miles were later marked both from this point and from Ashcroft, which makes the system confusing. Pavilion's Church of the Holy Trinity is well kept and still bears its original gingerbread crimping around the steeple.

Beside the church with its tumbled graveyard and children's playground, the old route leaves the highway and toils up to the summit of Pavilion Mountain in a series of steep switchbacks that play tag with the powerlines and rise steeply through sagebrush and open forests to a grassy plateau. On this huge expanse of unexpected tableland is the old Carson Ranch, now part of the Diamond S operations. Robert Carson was a Scot who came with his family to Ohio and joined a wagon train to Oregon when he was just 19. Lone survivor of an Indian massacre, he came north to try his luck in the gold rush. But as soon as he saw this land, so high and luxuriant with bunchgrass, he settled here and took up ranching, supplying hay and pigs to settlements along the way to the mines. Pavilion Mountain uplands release their winter snow grudgingly: the road is sometimes impassable as late as mid-May. Before you start this route, check road conditions at the Pavilion store or in Lillooet. If this section of road is not open, then keep on Highway 12 through Marble Canyon, turn north on Highway 97 to Clinton, then cut back and join the old route at Kelly Lake.

For years, even after the Fraser Canyon route was opened, hundreds of miners on foot or horseback, weekly stagecoaches and long lines of freight wagons toiled over Pavilion Mountain on their way to the gold camps of the Cariboo by way of Clinton. Last staging post before the summit was 29-Mile House, now vanished but the road can have changed little in the years between. It is narrow and winding and there are still long stretches of log fence, old and mossy, which must have watched the gold-rush traffic straggle by. On them at regular intervals today are nesting boxes for bluebirds. Sixteen kilometres from Pavilion, a sideroad leads to the summit forestry lookout and the road begins a swift and serpentine descent, dropping nearly 700 metres in less than six kilometres. So steep and dangerous was this section of the wagon road, known as the "Rattlesnake Grade", that freighters dragged logs behind them, to slow them down. If you stop here and peer over the edge, you can catch tantalizing glimpses through the trees of tiny Pear Lake, shaped like its name, twinkling far

Left: Alkali Lake Ranch, probably the oldest in B.C., a colourful cluster beside the road.

Right: The OK Ranch, formerly Haller's, one of the stopping places along the first River Trail to the Cariboo goldfields.

Opposite Page: The country road snakes through the meadows below Alkali Lake.

below the trees.

At the bottom of the hill, turn right for Kelly Lake and Clinton. Named for rancher Edward Kelly who settled here in 1866, this lovely lake completely fills the valley floor, skirted on one side by the road, on the other by the railway which comes in up Kelly Creek. At its northern end is Downing Provincial Park, a small and grassy campsite, a good place to listen for loons. Several pairs nest on the lake. Opposite the campsite, Kelly Lake Ranch offers trailrides and bed-and-breakfasts. Here the river trail leaves the wagon road route and today's main road to Clinton and turns up Porcupine Creek into a forested valley separated from the Fraser by the Edge Hills. Today, the road is signposted for Canoe Creek.

At 13 kilometres, birdwatchers will want to stop at the marshy ponds, good places to see nesting spotted sandpipers and to admire the view of the bald headed peaks of the Marble Range thrusting up above the forest. Past Limestone Mountain Ranch and the Circle H Mountain Lodge, the road leads on, ducking in and out of powerline clearings, to the settlement of Jesmond where the old Coldwell House sits behind a screen of hops. Jesmond was originally Mountain House, the name that the first settler Phil Grinder gave to the ranch he established here in 1870. In 1919 when Henry Coldwell opened a post-office in the ranch store, the government asked him to choose a more distinctive name for the settlement. Coldwell chose Jesmond, the name of his English birthplace. With all the wild roses round about, the winding road and the picturesque barns, Jesmond still has an Old World charm.

A signpost at a junction just beyond Jesmond directs travellers southwest for 19 kilometres to the Big Bar ferry across the Fraser, one of the few cable reaction ferries still running in the province. Where does the ferry lead? Only to logging roads on the far side of the river that four-wheel drivers on their way to Lillooet might like to try. The ferry, dating back to 1893, operates from April through November (closed for winter ice) and is on call from seven in the morning to seven at night, with breaks for lunch and dinner. The service, like others on the river, is free.

Just about opposite the road to the ferry another road takes off to the east and climbs high into the Marble Mountains to the alpine meadows around Jesmond Lookout. Unless prepared for a steep, rough and often muddy drive, this trip is better attempted on foot. It's a stiff ten kilometre hike but the views and the early summer wildflowers are great.

At 38 kilometres from Kelly Lake, Echo Springs Ranch offers fresh eggs for sale and beyond, the road crosses Big Bar Creek and enters the holdings of the OK Ranch. There's a large modern log house set back in the trees but of more interest are the old ranch buildings which huddle in a picturesque maze of log fences at the bottom of a curving dip in the road. Founded by Joseph Haller who came to B.C. in 1859, the ranch was known for years simply as Haller's and became the OK in 1933. The old buildings are deserted now but lilac still blooms around the door of the small frame homestead and there are usually swoops of swallows.

Beyond the ranch, the forests give way to rangeland, hilly and green and dotted with birch and pine. There are shallow lakes alive with nesting waterbirds and streams overflowing with the industry of beavers. A major intersection east leads to Big Bar Lake and out to Highway 97, a dull 45 kilometres along a wide but rough road. Keep north here and at the intersection to Meadow Lake a few kilometres farther (a second exit route to Highway 97) and head through Indian Meadows and into the tight canyon of Canoe Creek. Boxed in by limestone walls of ochre and grey, the blind corner here would make a perfect spot for an ambush.

The old Canoe Creek Indian village lies 16 kilometres beyond the Meadow Lake turnoff at the head of an expansive slope of irrigated fields. At the end of the valley, past the yellow ranchhouse and barns of the B.C. Cattle Company the road cuts through a high glacial esker, a steep and grassy knife-edged ridge that looks man-made. At the top, the River Trail finally begins its descent to the river. You will want to stop here. That first, fine, lonely view into the Fraser trench will amaze and delight. Below, the river coils peacefully through a huge expanse of wrinkled brown hills. The distance seems immense, the scale magnificent. A car at the bottom of the hill is only a speck of colour, a puff of dust; the road ahead merely a scratch. Apart from some fire-coloured cliffs on the far side of the river the colours are sombre, for most of the land is sagebrush, grey and drab in summer. Any colours there are seem flagrant: a tuft of flowering rabbitbrush in August, the flame of a fall aspen, the green edges of an irrigation ditch or a cultivated meadow.

After this first heady swoop down from the plateau, the road runs for 15 kilometres along the broken benchlands of the Fraser, a circuitous route through sandy sagebrush, past cliffs of wind-licked sand and volcanic outcrops, in and out of steep dry

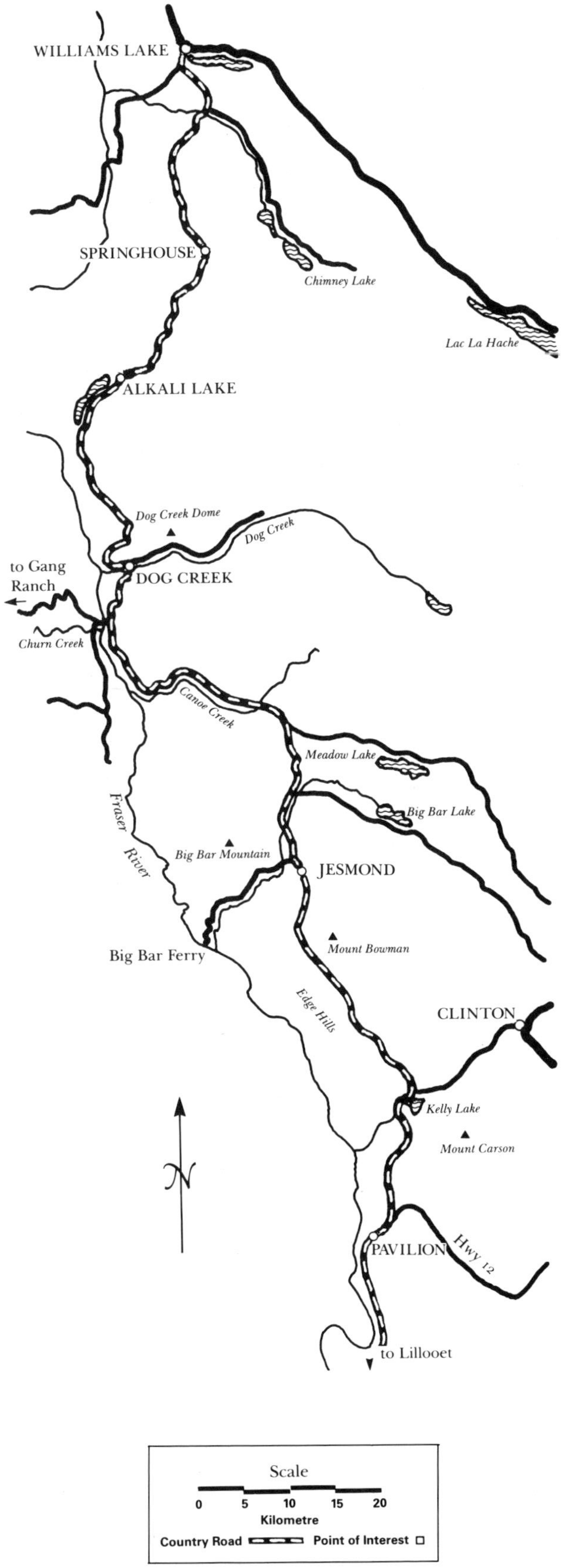

gulches where stands of twisted pine provide little shade, alongside a large meadow planted with blue-green alfalfa. It is only at times that you catch a glimpse of the river, surging silently at the bottom of its deep furrow, yet all the landscape here was modelled by water. It was glacial meltwater sluicing down from the receding glaciers of the Ice Age that first cut the Fraser Trench into the volcanic rocks of the plateau. Thousands of years of erosion from tributary streams, plus eons of wind and rain have added further refinements. On the bluffs above the Churn Creek bridge the river is close; you can hear it roar.

Where Churn Creek gushes into the Fraser just south of the bridge it has created a little delta, green with willows and cottonwoods, that makes a grand picnic site. The road across the river leads to the great cattle ranches of the Gang and Empire Valley. The Gang Ranch, so named because it was the first in the area to use the double-furrowed gang plough, was founded by the Harper brothers in 1883 and it is the largest by area in North America. If you go this way you will reach, by way of Farwell Canyon, the Chilcotin Highway near Riske Creek.

Above the bridge, the River Trail strikes away from the river, climbing steeply up onto a dry forested plateau that in May is yellow with sunflowers, then down again into the green hollow of Dog Creek, about eight kilometres north. Dog Creek community claims to be one of the oldest in the Interior of B.C, founded in 1856 when a hotel was built here to cater to the traffic on the River Trail. The hotel advertised "the finest wines, liquor and cigars", provided stables for 25 horses and was the headquarters for the Dog Creek Stagelines, the first to be officially licensed in B.C. Long after the River Trail was abandoned in favour of the wagon road, and even long after the wagon road became a highway, the Dog Creek Stage continued to run, though by the 1970s it was a sturdy blue bus that made the twice-weekly trips to Williams Lake. Dog Creek also had the first flour mill in the mainland, built in 1866, and a water-driven sawmill owned by a French nobleman, the Count of Versepeuch (also known as Gaspar) who built here a substantial house and reputedly traded his elegant court clothes—his tri-corned hat and blue satin jacket—with Indian Chief Alexis for a string of horses.

Alas for Dog Creek! The two storey log building that served for so long as a fascinating general store and post-office, dispensing gasoline from its creaking pumps, closed down in the mid 1980s, along with the Dog Creek Stage. This scenic crossroads used to be one of the highlights of the trip, a

In May, the meadows and roadsides are thick with wildflowers. Right: the gold of oysterplant; below: the sharp yellow-green of leafy spurge.

Above: The Fraser River surges through its deep trench and above it, on benches thick with sagebrush, the road runs through to Dog Creek.

chance to stop and chat and buy refreshments. Today, out of habit perhaps, it is still a mandatory stop, if only to search in the bushes for relics of the old mill, to watch for bluebirds, mourning doves and lazuli buntings, to listen to the meadowlarks.

Indians lived at Dog Creek long before the Europeans came. They live here still: a sharp right turn here will take you several kilometres to their village with its pretty white church, store and gas station. And in a huge cavern at the foot of the sheer basaltic escarpment which marks the eastern edge of Dog Creek Dome on the north side of the valley there are prehistoric pictographs. Painted in red ochre, they show mostly men but there is also a dog and perhaps a ruffed grouse. The cave, despite its three metre height and 70-metre-wide mouth, is hard to locate and requires a steep uncomfortable scramble up the scree slopes beneath the cliffs.

The road that follows Dog Creek past the Indian village eventually joins Highway 97 at the railway flag stop of Enterprise, but except for the first several kilometres the road is wide, straight and uninteresting, built primarily for logging trucks. It is better by far to continue on the River Trail which climbs back out of the valley and up onto high benchland above the river, where in summer, among the sagebrush, you can find numbers of Mariposa lilies, their delicate flowers like three-petalled tulips in a pale shade of lavender. The derelict ruins of Captain Meason's ranch, founded in 1879, stand gaunt on the canyon lip. The big house burned; only a couple of old cabins and a corral remains of this historic spread which once stretched for 25 kilometres along the river.

As the road continues to climb to cooler elevations, pines return to shelter the landscape and in spring the gold of sunflowers shines beneath the trees. About 30 kilometres from Dog Creek, the road heads east away from the river towards Alkali Lake, running through irrigated fields of barley and alfalfa, all beautifully green in early summer. The lake has been set aside as the Riedemann Wildlife Sanctuary and birdlife on the water and in the fields and shrubbery around the perimeter is rich and varied. Here you stand a good chance of seeing some of B.C.'s white pelicans which nest only in a small colony at Stum Lake northeast of Alexis Creek and which fly through on migration. Northern orioles, bobolinks and long-billed curlews are three other splendid birds to watch for here.

Alkali Lake Ranch at the head of the valley is a photogenic arrangement of squared log barns and brilliant red roofs lining both sides of the road. Started in 1861 on the site of a former River Trail roadhouse, it claims to be the oldest cattle ranch in the province. It is certainly one of the prettiest. The ranchhouse itself is old and substantial, surrounded by spacious lawns and set apart from the road along a driveway lined by tall poplars. There used to be a store and post office in a little log house (complete with hitching post) beside the driveway, but this is closed now and for supplies the Indian village on the bluff above the road satisfies local requirements.

Beyond the village, the countryside becomes gradually more domestic; the meadows are smaller and greener and there are more trees. At 24 kilometres from Alkali Lake the gravel road turns to pavement, tempting you to hurry along. But the road is not over yet: there are several more lakes, one an ecological reserve, the scattered community of Springhouse with its old school, air park, guest ranch and long stretches of Russell fence, and another sideroad to explore. This one leads up Chimney Creek to Brunson, Felker and Chimney Lakes, known to birders for sightings of sandhill cranes, and eventually meets up with the Dog Creek-Enterprise road. The lakes have campgrounds, good fishing, and a small colony of recreational homes, for the road is now close to civilization. It's only another ten kilometres down the River Trail, now wide and well used, to Highway 20, just east of Williams Lake.

SODA CREEK CIRCUIT

There are some settlements, woven early into the strands of history, that are discarded when changing fortune refutes the reason for their being. A mine runs out of ore; a bypass road is built; a railway pushes through or is closed down; the river boat's whistle is silent. Faced with drastic change to its economy, the settlement may ultimately die, a natural process in the survival of the fittest, a law that works quickly when man's hand is involved.

The Cariboo gold rush forged the first tenuous link from British Columbia's coast to the Interior, spawning settlements and supply stations along the way and leaving, when it was over, a debris of broken and deserted places. Some of these have survived, prospering with the changing times, but many others sank slowly into oblivion, earth to earth, ashes to ashes. Then there are those that linger on: not dead but certainly forgotten.

Soda Creek is one such town, a shadow of its former self. On the Fraser River at the start of easy navigation, it was for a time the terminus of the first Cariboo wagon road. All the hopeful traffic bound for Barkerville and the gold mines poured into the town where they transferred, after a boisterous wait, to paddlewheelers for the journey upriver to Quesnel and the last rough haul. When the gold rush was finished, Soda Creek continued to thrive as the start of navigation up the Fraser to Prince George and points north. For 60 years, before the building of railways and roads into the northcountry, the river settlement was a vital link in the opening up of northern British Columbia. Here were hotels and boarding houses, mills for flour and lumber, general stores, a school, a church and all the paraphernalia of an important supply centre. Today, it's hardly on the map, well away from the highway. It has no store, no gas station. There is little reason beside curiosity and a feeling for history to make the journey.

Soda Creek can be the focus for a circle tour that leads into the Fraser River country north of Williams Lake where one of the few remaining reaction ferries and a once privately-owned bridge allow a choice of cross-river loops. Once over the river, you can meander pleasantly through the ranchlands to Meldrum Creek and out onto the Bella Coola Road, a round trip which can be accomplished pleasantly in half a day from Williams Lake.

Like the wagon road that preceded it, Highway 97 bypasses the centre of Williams Lake, turning away from the river onto the jackpine highlands. You can reach Soda Creek from a highway connection farther north but the more leisurely way—and the prettier—is to follow the river. Drive along the main street of Williams Lake to the railway station, recently converted into an art gallery. The Soda Creek Road leads upriver past the cemetery, clinging to the edge of the Fraser's great trench.

At first the road's surroundings are suburban,

Top: Lilac shrouds an old cabin at Soda Creek, a former steamboat settlement on the Fraser.

Bottom: The ferry at Marguerite.

The eroded sandy cliffs beside the Chilcotin River at Farwell Canyon: castles in the air.

then industrial, with sawmills and stacks of logs to remind you of the local importance of the forest industry. But by seven kilometres you're out into the country, the forests bright in May with sunflowers and chokecherry blossoms, in August with the pale yellow of the oysterplant. Almost immediately the road climbs precariously onto a high rock bluff and you see the river far below in all its thick brown strength. Now you're on the plateau and the forest gives way to benchland carpeted with fields of alfalfa. The river, out of sight, is marked only by a line of eroded sandstone cliffs.

About 20 kilometres along, Buckskin Road enters from the west. This leads down to a bridge across the river, once the only privately-owned toll bridge in B.C. Rancher Rudy Johnson of the Buckskin Ranch on the river's west side grew tired of making the 60-kilometre trip to town along dusty backroads by way of Meldrum Creek, so he bought a second-hand bridge and had it erected here in 1968. The steel bridge cost him $40,000; transportation and assembly on two concrete piers brought the price up to more than $200,000 but it reduced Johnson's road distance to Williams Lake to less than 25 kilometres, saving him both time and gas. Of course, he let others use his shortcut and defrayed some of his costs by charging commercial vehicles (mostly logging trucks) a toll.

Recently, however, the provincial government bought the bridge from Johnson and it is now part of the highway system. On past occasions the road to Soda Creek along the river has been closed because of washouts and we have been glad to use Johnson's bridge as a detour, crossing back over the river on the Soda Creek ferry. But this service, the oldest ferry in B.C.—it began operations in 1868—stopped running in 1978. The next crossing upriver is the ferry at Marguerite.

Continue on the road to Soda Creek, through large hayfields beside the Fraser where giant irrigation pumps make rainbow arches and dowse the roadside shrubbery, past old barns and ranchhouses, past haystacks like giant loaves of bread. The road ducks underneath the railway and then climbs in and out of the deep gash of Hawks Creek (formerly Deep Creek). At about 30 kilometres a well-travelled road leads east through Indian reserve lands to Highway 97. This is the route of the first Cariboo wagon road as it came down from 150 Mile House. Shortly you will cross the creek that gave Soda Creek its name—the water, passing through a limestone rock formation, is bubbly as if carbonated. The clay banks of the creek here are pitted with swallow holes.

The settlement of Soda Creek lies ahead down a dead-end road. Here the Fraser changes character, leaving its rapids and horrendous gorges for a wide trench and a steady surge, well suited to navigation. The first wagon road of 1863 ended here and G.B. Wright who had built the road up from Clinton ordered a steamboat built, the S.S. Enterprise, to transport men and supplies upriver the rest of the way to Quesnel.

That same year Dr. Walter Cheadle and Viscount William Milton made their epic journey to the Cariboo. Out from England for a walk across Canada, they were B.C.'s first real tourists and left an entertaining account of their travels. They reported that: "The boat was built on the river, all the timber sawn by hand, the shaft in five pieces packed on mules, cylinders in two, boiler plates brought in same manner. Boat cost $75,000."

It took about 24 hours for the little Enterprise to battle the river currents to Quesnel, but less than three hours for the return trip. The boat ran for eight years between Soda Creek and Quesnel, then went north to work on the lakes system north of Fort St. James. In all, some nine different ships sailed out of Soda Creek, providing continuous service upriver until 1921.

Soda Creek today consists of one main road angling down to the river, with at least one beautiful old log house, several newer ones and lots of empty gaps between. At the end of the road, shaded by cottonwood trees, a large building emblazoned with the title "Soda Creek Hall Social Club Inc." suggests that the ostensibly sleepy little community beats with a lively heart. In spring, the settlement is green and blooming; there are great mounds of lilac, flowering fruit trees, pretty flower gardens—an air of lush abandon. And the river rushes by, impervious to its forgotten past.

It is interesting to trace the changing fortunes of this little town. An early traveller John Macoun, botanist on the Sir Sandford Fleming expedition across the Rockies to find a railway route in the 1850s, described it as having "two taverns, two grist and one sawmill on the creek" and commented that "the mill at Soda Creek makes excellent flour". Ten years later Cheadle and Milton described the miners who came down from Barkerville: "The steamer came in about two o'clock bringing a host of miners, two of whom were very drunk and continued to imbibe every five minutes. During the time we stayed in the house they must have had 20 drinks. The swearing was something fearful". The "house" the English tourists stayed in while waiting for the stage was probably the large log Colonial House, built and operated by Peter Dunlevy, finder of the first gold in the Cariboo.

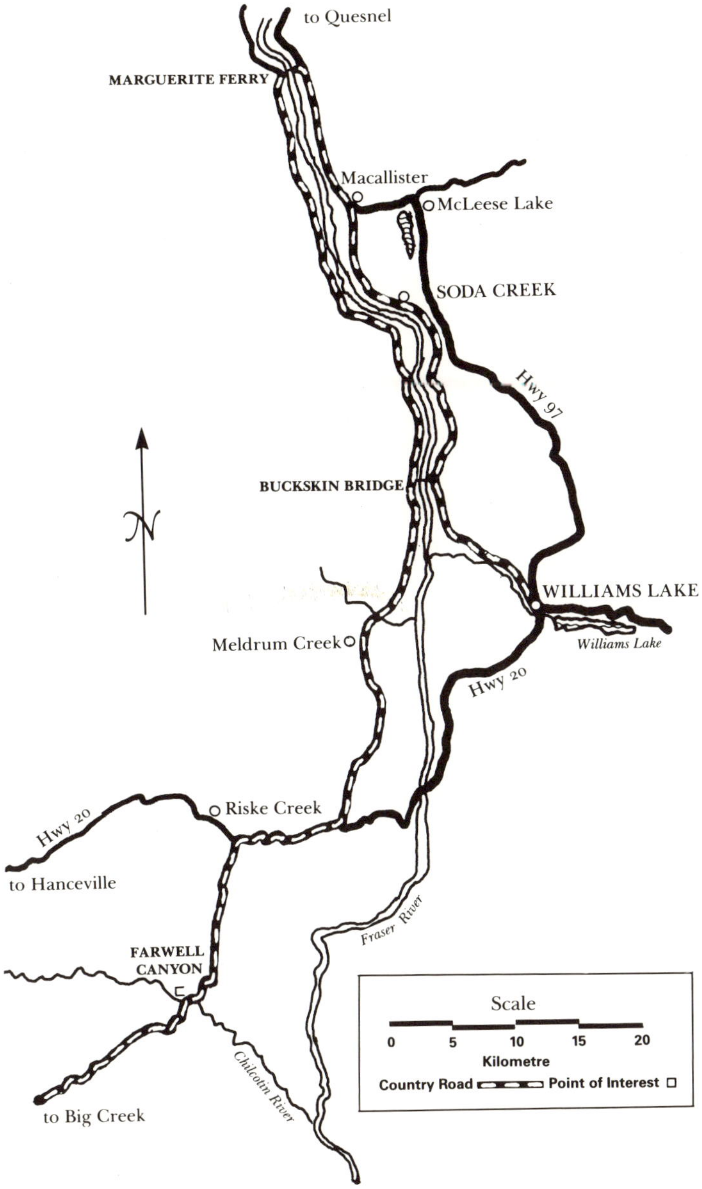

By 1882, according to the B.C. Directory, there were two hotels here, stores, a telegraph office and post office; Hawks and Collins ran the flour mill. Among the 24 residents listed were a stagedriver, a teamster and a river pilot, plus 14 farmers whose address was simply "Chilcoten". Eleven years later the Directory described Soda Creek as a village on the stage route from Ashcroft to Barkerville with weekly mail service and semi-weekly trips to Quesnel on the steamships. It also mentioned its "steel cable ferry with larger scow, a great convenience for farmers and tourists going to the Chilcoten". Population was 75 and the village had a resident doctor.

In 1910 the Directory remarked on the thrice weekly stages from Ashcroft and the steamers for Fort George. Population included a master mariner and a teacher. By 1923 Soda Creek had a station on the nearby Pacific Great Eastern Railway (now the B.C. Railway); it had telephone connections, a public school, a Roman Catholic church and an Indian reserve. The river boats had gone, pushed aside by the railway they helped to build. Was this Soda Creek's heyday?

In 1945 there were 175 residents, including two ferrymen; the flour mill was still operating and the community boasted of its "Everglades Country Club". But by 1951 a tourist account of the village described it as "little more than a couple of primitive stores and a gas station". Today, even these are gone and it seems that, of the old days, only the lilacs remain.

The best view of Soda Creek and the most compelling atmosphere of the past may be had from the road which climbs up behind the village on a higher bench of land on its way north. Past the Centennial cairn, stop and look back over the top of a sod-roofed cabin smothered in blackberry and lilac. The curve of the river below, the gleam of the clay banks on the opposite shore, the old wagon road snaking "down, down the swift descent of Soda Creek hill" create a view that is fine indeed. Farther along this road is the cemetery. On the river side are unmarked graves stoutly defended by wooden pickets in a tangle of wild grass. Across the road, semblances of a more formal Victorian graveyard can be found, with several elegant monuments, one a draped marble obelisk in memory of Captain Frank Odin of the Steamship Charlotte who died here in 1899. The graveyard is shaded by giant pines, flowered with violets and wild strawberries, a peaceful place indeed.

Continue north along this road through the hayfields and irrigated meadows of large ranches (one is named the Dr. Dunlevy Ranch and has a lovely old-fashioned frame farmhouse). Eight kilometres beyond Soda Creek you can visit the site of the old ferry crossing, then continue north, enjoying the serenity of the countryside, for another 12 kilometres to a railway overpass and a junction with Highway 97 at the whistle stop of Macalister. From here you have no choice but to follow the highway, either south back to Williams Lake or north about 10 kilometres to the Marguerite ferry.

This is a cable reaction ferry, identical to the one that used to operate near Soda Creek—in fact it is the old Soda Creek ferry, rebuilt. The service runs on call from 7 in the morning to 7 at night, but closes down for an hour at lunchtime and supper time. Its power comes from the river's own current and there's a strong overhead cable to keep it

The rich meadows of the Chilcotin near Riske Creek provide rangeland for cattle.

Below: Chilcotin roads are briefly brilliant with spring dandelions.

Bottom: An old ranch lies safe in the arms of the Chilcotin River at Farwell Canyon, its little meadow pricked out in wild mustard.

on course and prevent it from being swept downstream. There are several such ferries operating in B.C., mostly on the Fraser and the North Thompson, and anchor cables have been known to break and ferries to be cast adrift, but don't let this worry you. Enjoy your trip across the river. (Marguerite was named after an Indian woman said to have drowned several of her unwanted babies in a nearby lake.)

On the west side of the Fraser, the gravel road goes north by way of Narcosli Creek all the way to Quesnel. Turn south to complete a circular return route to Williams Lake. The road meanders through the jackpines past the road leading to the old Soda Creek ferry and intersects with Buckskin Road which leads down to Rudy Johnson's Bridge. Decide if you want to return to Williams Lake this way. If not continue on through ranch country to Meldrum Creek, about 20 kilometres from the bridge turning. From this loosely knit community it's another 20 kilometres out through open country dotted with lakes onto Highway 20, the Chilcotin Highway. Turn left (east) here for a scenic and speedy drive back to Williams Lake.

Notice the nesting boxes set up for bluebirds on fenceposts beside the road. The boxes are situated in pairs because one is sure to be claimed by tree swallows, which nest earlier. The swallows won't let another swallow take over the second box but apparently don't mind bluebirds for neighbours because they don't compete for exactly the same insects.

Side Trip

If you have time to spare, turn west instead of east along the Chilcotin Highway, drive for 11.5 kilometres, then turn south along a sideroad signposted for Big Creek. This will lead through the green meadows and scattered dwellings of Toosey Indian village and off across the plateau towards the Chilcotin River. Thirteen kilometres along, the land falls away suddenly into a deep trench and the road corkscrews down into yawning Farwell Canyon, its yellow clay banks fretted into spires and steeples and hoodoos. Below, the river churns, milky green with sediment, in a great sinuous loop. The road crosses the river on a one-lane wooden bridge then zig-zags laboriously up again onto the thickly treed Fraser plateau. You can drive on, if you choose, all the way west to Big Creek, then north to the highway again at Lee's Corner, a forest drive of 60 kilometres or so along a dusty road. But if you're like us, Farwell Canyon itself is a compelling destination.

The Chilcotin is a wild river, beloved of whitewater kayakers, rafters and fishermen. Along its banks here a herd of 400 bighorn sheep, perhaps a fifth of the world's total population, makes its home. And cuddled in the arms of the river under those stupendous towers of clay lies a lovely little ranch, its meadow embroidered ever so lightly with wild mustard. It's a beautiful place, ideal for a picnic or a hike. Shuswap Indians used to live here but the smallpox epidemic of 1862 killed them all. Their village sites on both sides of the river can now hardly be distinguished but the people left tangible signs of their presence. Look for pictographs on an overhanging rock on the benchland just south of the bridge.

There's just one thing that could spoil the canyon for you. The Big Creek road is at times a major route for logging trucks. If they are on the road, raising clouds of choking dust and drowning out the chatter of the river, then you won't want to stay for more than a minute.

FOOTHILLS JOURNEY

Some of the loveliest scenery in Alberta lies in the southwest corner, where the plains swell briefly into foothills before the grand crescendo of the mountains themselves: the snow-crowned towers of Waterton Lakes National Park. There are two main routes into Waterton: Highway 6 south from Pincher Creek and Highway 5 west from Cardston, both scenic drives in themselves, and between them the countryside is laced with smaller country roads that invite dalliance. The route we chose begins in Pincher Creek and wends its way through the foothills to Police Outpost, a provincial park smack on the border with Montana. It's a route for collectors of abandoned schoolhouses, old churches, ghost towns—and superb mountain views.

Pincher Creek is a pleasant little town snuggled down beside the creek where in 1874 a pair of pincers, lost six years earlier by prospectors, was found again. It was the site of a North West Mounted Police post in 1878 and history buffs will want to visit the museum and the cabin of famed frontiersman, Kootenai Brown. From Highway 6 in Pincher Creek, take Secondary Road 507 and head east through relatively flat farmland.

Country roads everywhere in the Alberta prairies are section roads, following the compass directions of a gridwork established by surveyors around the turn of the century when they carved up the land for settlement. The roads go straight, heedless of minor obstacles such as hills, and only stop in their tracks for totally impassable geological features such as lakes, wide rivers or sheer cliffs. In the general scheme of things there are usually roads, or tracks or at least fencelines at every mile. If you're familiar with the system, you don't need to look at your odometer.

At 15.5 kilometres along Secondary 507, Road 786 comes in from Brocket in the north and 507 veers abruptly south for two notches in the grid to avoid a steep escarpment, then turns east again. Just before the turn is the abandoned community schoolhouse at Halifax, painted red, with two little outhouses and a stack of busy beehives in the yard behind. At the next right-angle bend, a signpost to Fishburn invites a turn south along an unpaved section road that cuts straight across the grain of the landscape, slicing up hill and down again to keep true to its survey. From the crests of the hills, the mountain views are marvellous.

Fishburn is one of those tantalizing ghost towns that have vanished almost without a trace. Described in a 1901 police report as "located on the dry fork of the Kootenay" (today's Foothill Creek) and "the centre of a thriving settlement", it was of sufficient size to have a post office as early as 1894. Named after the first settler, A.M. Fish, all that is left of the town today is the church, standing alone with its single tree and its well-tended graves just to the east of the road (turn off at around 26 kilometres.) A nearby little lake is a good spot to watch red-winged and yellow-headed blackbirds busy in the tules.

Keep going south on the section road, ignoring a right turn signposted to Highway 6. Just before joining Secondary Road 505, turn left (east) for a visit to another abandoned school, perhaps the most melancholy one of all for it was called Utopia. A wrought iron sign records its birth in the promised land in 1904 and its death in 1950. Behind the schoolhouse, the land falls away steeply to the great reservoir formed by the dam across the Waterton River. In June, the back slope is brilliant gold with balsamroot sunflowers, a glory the children must have loved, and on the horizon, the square hatchet-face of Chief Mountain looms blue.

Even section roads have to yield to the Waterton reservoir. Continue east then south to join

Above: Buffalo in Waterton.

Right: St Henry's Church, north of Twin Butte.

Top: In the southern Alberta foothills, two seasons and two geographies meet: fall harvest on the plains and winter snow in the mountains.

Top: The pioneer church of St. Stephen in a fold of the lonely hills.

Above: Fishing below the Waterton Reservoir spillway.

Left: A woodland trail beside Outpost Lake.

Highway 505 which will lead you over the dam and spillway at the north end of the huge man-made lake. But if you are interested in churches, detour briefly west along Highway 505. You'll see St. Henry's church from far off: it tops a ridge above the railway spur at Drywood. Seen against the Rocky Mountains, its red Gothic spire and roof form a distant and somehow European vignette, something out of Switzerland, perhaps.

The dam and the reservoir are well worth a stop, if only to admire the view. Immediately over the spillway, turn north and wind down below the dam to the original river at the base of the spillway, a giant waterslide. Anglers might want to fish here in the pool beneath the spillway and geologists will be interested in the folded rock strata of the river cliffs. It's a good place for a picnic, if you can tear yourself away from the emerald waters of the reservoir. Swallows by the hundreds nest under the bridge here and it's a likely spot to see white pelicans.

Beyond the reservoir, turn south and follow Road 800 (it is aimed like an arrow directly at Chief Mountain) to the village of Hill Spring, founded in 1911 and named for a nearby spring whose water today is piped into the community. You can see the spring on a hillside just to the north of the village. It's a quiet place with welcome shade trees and there's a good little cafe, the Crackerbarrel, near the end of the main street. Here, too, is all that remains of the village schoolhouse: the bell, set up on a little tower and with a simple epitaph "1913 to 1965".

Follow the road south of Hill Spring, still with Chief Mountain in your sights. This landmark, a dominant mountain block set a little apart from the main range, lies just to the south of the U.S.-Canada boundary line. The road angles a bit to cross the Belly River and cuts across a corner of the Blood Indian Reserve, the largest in Canada, which stretches between the Belly, St. Mary's and Oldman rivers, southwest of Lethbridge. All this was once illegal whisky-trading country. Northeast near the Belly Buttes where the Blood Indians still hold their spectacular sun dances at the time of the summer solstice, are the sites of Stand-Off and Fort Kipp, trading posts put out of business when the stalwart redcoats of the North West Mounted Police trekked west to bring British law and order—and prohibition for the Indians—to this part of the British Empire.

At about 60 kilometres from Pincher Creek, Road 800 meets Highway 5 from Cardston. If your destination is Waterton, then turn west here and continue into the park. Otherwise turn east and

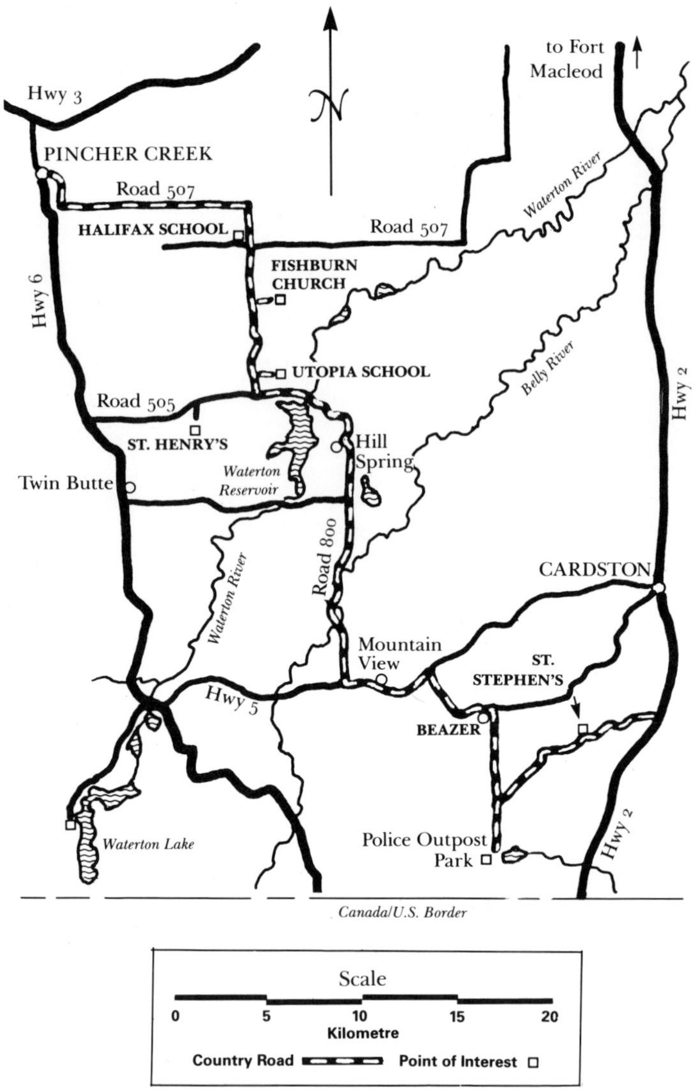

head for the village of Mountain View, founded in 1895 by Mormon settlers. Its name is apt: it's hard to imagine a lovelier view of the mountains than this one, framed by farm fields. The Church of Latter Day Saints is by far the biggest and newest building in the village but of more interest, perhaps, is a tourist store and cafe beside Caribou Clothes, a factory for local sheepskin wear. The road outside is lined with old weather-beaten wagons.

The far southwestern corner of Alberta is Mormon country. Charles Ora Card in 1887 led the members of his church here by wagon train all the way from Salt Lake City, crossing the border at nearby Immigrant Gap. He founded the city, named in his honour, and he built a great white granite temple, the first Mormon church in the British Empire. Traditionally polygamous, the Mormons had to promise to bring with them only one wife apiece before they were allowed to settle in Canada. From their centre at Cardston, splinter groups spread out to establish other communities. Mountain View was one of these. By 1898 it had a creamery, a carpenter's shop and a smithy, and later equipment was brought in from Utah to run a cheese factory.

Four kilometres east of Mountain View, just past a small lake, a road branches southwest signposted to Police Outpost Provincial Park. This is the way to another old Mormon settlement called Beazer, today a ghost town of tumble-down log buildings almost hidden in the poplars beside Lee Creek. From Beazer, the road strikes due south for Outpost Lake just north of the U.S. border, site of a lonely North West Mounted Police post. The boundary here was regularly patrolled from 1891 to 1899, perilous years of Indian unrest, rum running and cattle rustling that also saw the beginning of Alberta settlement. The actual site of the police post and its log house, kitchen, stables, oatshed and corrals, known to be somewhere on the southeast corner of the lake, has never been found.

The park around the lake under the watchful eye of the Chief is noted for the variety and abundance of its wildflowers. In addition to dry prairie and hill species, there are forest flowers such as wintergreen and wild orchids. The lake's little island is accessible by footbridge and there are several short hiking trails, as well as camp and picnic sites, boat launch and gravel beaches. The lake is kept stocked with rainbow trout. Except for summer weekends when it is overrun with fishermen in powerboats, it is a lonely spot. But how much lonelier it must have been 90 years ago when the three men posted here, the sole representatives of British law and government, were several days' hard ride from the tiny speck of civilization called Fort Macleod.

Adjacent to the park is Outpost Wetlands Natural Area in the marshlands around Boundary Creek, a good spot for nature study of all kinds but particularly for birds, including such rarities as the sandhill crane, cinnamon teal and northern waterthrush.

The quickest route from Police Outpost to Cardston heads east about half way back towards Beazer and runs a zig-zag course northeast (no section line road this) over the hills to meet Highway 2 south of the city. En route it passes another of Alberta's lovely pioneer churches, one of the province's oldest. The white-painted church of St. Stephen was built on South Hill in 1901 and rebuilt on its present scenic spot in a fold of the hills in 1907. Its pioneer cemetery is a good place to end the day—and this country road.

ALONG THE WILD WEST COAST

Vancouver Island's western edge is rocky and wild, bearing the brunt of fierce Pacific storms and deluges of rain. Where the land meets the sea it has been broken down into islands and rocky promontories, hidden reefs and undersea ledges, scooped out into bays and torn by long inlets. Shrouded by frequent fog banks, the land itself is—or was—impenetrable, a dense mantle of rainforest covering the granite knees and elbows of some of the ruggedest mountains on earth.

The West Coast Trail was built originally as a lifeline for shipwreck survivors along a section of the coast known as the Graveyard of the Pacific and every summer it lures an influx of stalwart hikers eager for a five-day wilderness endurance test. To reach the trail's southern start hikers must first negotiate a hundred kilometres of road along the coast from Victoria, a journey that must seem tame indeed compared to the perils of the trail itself. But for less rugged travellers, the West Coast Road can be adventurous enough. It is narrow and curvy and it leads to so many interesting places that it provides more than enough entertainment for a day trip out from Victoria. There are several beautiful beaches, great views across the strait to the mountains of Washington's Olympic Peninsula, logging road side-trips, wild streams and deep forests, lighthouses, and a good smattering of history—a perfect combination for a country road.

From Victoria, head out on Highway 1 and branch onto Highway 14 near the head of Esquimalt Inlet. This first section of road to Metchosin and Sooke was built as a carriage road in 1872 to link pioneer farms and settlements along the warm southwest coast. But from Sooke north, a road connection was not completed until 1957. Of the old stage road there are two very good reminders: the old coaching inns at Six-Mile and 17-Mile, both very Tudor in aspect, and both still open for business. For history in a large gulp, turn off the road at Colwood and follow the signs to Fort Rodd Hill, built in 1895 to defend the naval base in Esquimalt Harbour across the bay. A National Historic Park, the fort's well-tended remains lie within a huge expanse of scenic rocky parkland typical of the east coast rainshadow, a marvellous place for a stroll. Fisgard Lighthouse, built of bricks brought around the horn as ballast in sailing ships, is connected to the fort by a causeway and has been on guard here since 1860. If there are children in your party, the fort and the lighthouse will occupy them for hours; they may not want to leave at all.

From the fort double back a way and turn left (west) onto Ocean Boulevard down to Esquimalt Lagoon, a federal bird sanctuary known for the numbers of black brant geese which winter here. At the head of the lagoon lie the nurtured grounds of Hatley Park (open to the public) and Royal Roads Military college. The road crosses a hump-backed bridge and threads the spit of land between the lagoon and the sea.

Opposite Page: A beach of one's own at Sandcut along the West Coast Road. Above: The Sandcut waterfalls.

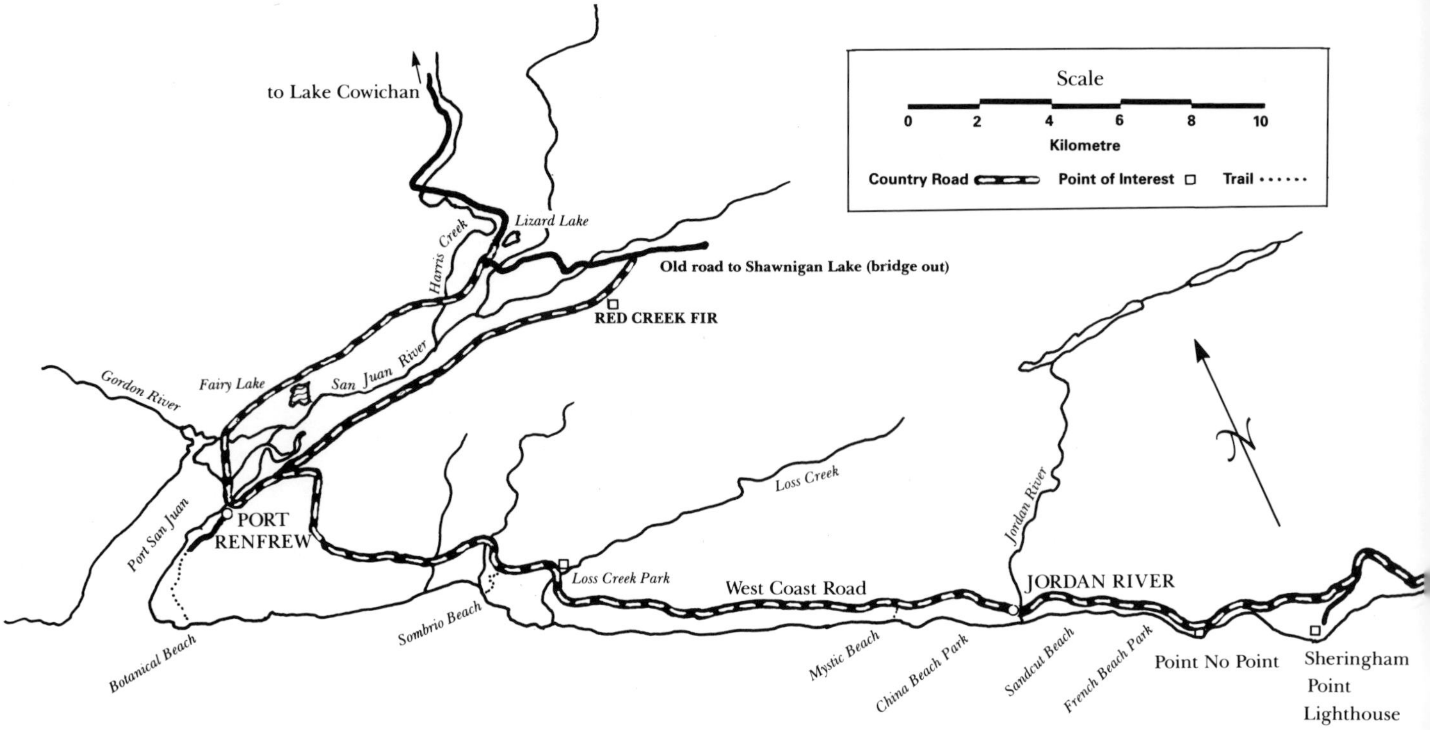

Continue along the spit, turning inland along Lagoon Road, then left (north) on Metchosin Road. Birdwatchers will want to wheel in to Witty's Lagoon Park, a short distance along.

In the heart of Metchosin just before the intersection of Happy Valley Road lies the tiny Anglican church of St. Mary the Virgin, built in 1873. Impeccably dresed out in black and white, the church is fondly known as St. Mary's of the Lilies because in April the surrounding graveyard shaded by ancient gary oaks is smothered in the delicate white nodding heads of erythroniums, known locally as Easter lilies. In summer, wild white daisies take their place. It is an enchanting spot. A little way up Happy Valley Road lies the pioneer school, built in 1872.

You can continue along this road all the way back to Highway 14 or turn left on Rocky Point and take a more direct line up Kangaroo Road. At the Rocky Point intersection is an access point for a fascinating regional park—one that is 47 kilometres long and only 30 metres wide. This is the abandoned roadbed of the CN Railway, fondly known as the Galloping Goose, which went from View Royal near Victoria to the head of Sooke Basin and up Sooke River. Canada's first "Rails to Trails" conversion, this linear trail is popular with hikers, cyclists and horseback riders and hopefully will set a good example for other railway trails in Western Canada.

Highway 14, the old Sooke Road, meanders around the north side of Sooke Basin. At the bridge over the Sooke River lies the old Milne homestead built in 1888 and the excellent Sooke regional museum. Edward Milne opened a store here in 1893 and built a wharf so he could bring in his goods by sea and the area is still known as Milne's Landing. The Sooke Potholes upriver a way are well worth a visit for summer swimming. Farther upstream (though not accessible by this road, which is gated) lies the site of the gold discoveries at Leechtown which prompted a local but ephemeral goldrush back in 1864. Today, the most interesting way to the goldfields is by foot or bike along the Galloping Goose Trail, about ten kilometres.

Sooke itself was first claimed as Spanish territory; Manuel Quimper in 1792 named the bay Porto de Nevillo Cigado and took possession in the name of the king of Spain. Six years later, Spain withdrew her claim to the coast of B.C. and the area was surveyed again by the British who gave British names to everything in sight except for Sooke itself which already had an Indian name. At Maple Avenue, which leads down to the government wharf, a cairn commemorates the landing of the first settler, William Grant, who established a homestead here in 1849, bringing with him from Scotland eight other workers. He stayed only a brief time but he left a legacy impossible to ignore.

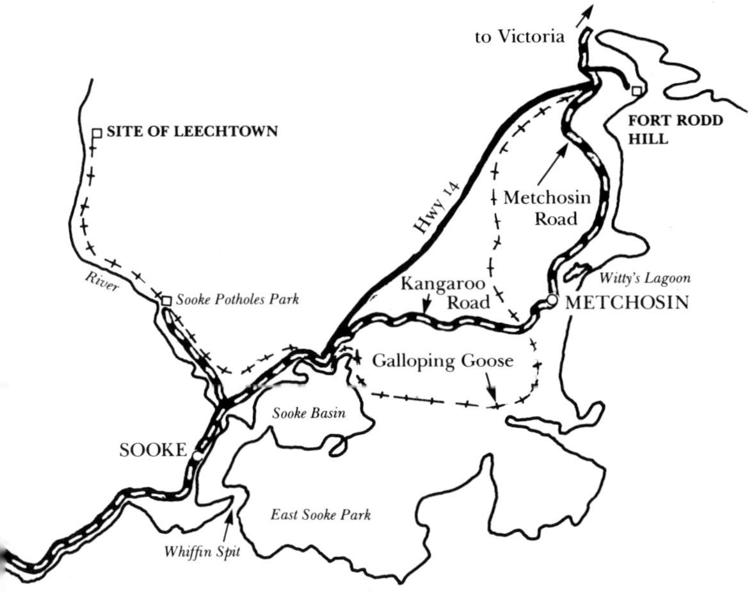

On his Sooke estate he planted seeds of English broom, a tough little plant which flourished and spread like wildfire, distributing touches of bright gold all over southern Vancouver Island. The hill above the harbour is called Broom Hill in memory of Grant's gift while Mount Manuel Quimper, higher and to the east, surveys all the basin that its namesake once claimed for Spain.

Just beyond the village Whiffin Spit Road leads down to a remarkable strip of land that almost seals off the bay from the ocean. This natural breakwater provides excellent bird-watching, clamming, picnics and other activities and nearby Sooke Harbour House has become world famous for its cuisine which uses fresh herbs and vegetables from its own seaside garden.

Beyond Whiffin Spit, the winding road continues along the shore although the sea views are mostly obscured by second growth forest. At Gordon Beach, however, there's a fine shingle strand and a great panorama across the Strait of Juan de Fuca to the Olympic Mountains of Washington. From here to Port Renfrew there are beaches all the way but the road for the most part was built well back from the coast and beach expeditions require descents through the forest on trails of varying degrees of steepness and slipperyness. The rougher the trail though, the better the chance of having a stretch of beach all to yourself even in midsummer.

At Shirley, founded in 1885 as an agricultural settlement, turn left at the community hall for Sheringham Point Lighthouse. The installation, now fully automated, is closed to the public but trails lead out onto the headland for a fine view of the light, built in 1912. The wooded bluffs are a great place for a picnic. Look for chocolate lilies here in early May.

Just past the point, the road returns close to the coast and French Beach provincial park nearby provides good camp and beach facilities, and whale-watching in spring and fall for migrating grays. It's possible to launch canoes and kayaks here for a closer look at the whales and for river otters, seals and sealions. Another scenic lookout is at Point No Point where a teahouse offers light lunches, afternoon teas and accommodations in little cliff-top cottages. The point acquired its odd name because when the coast was first surveyed the prominent headland here was seen from one survey station, but appeared non-existent from another. The 1895 survey called it Glacier Point, but it was changed back in 1957. Just beyond Point No Point is a parking lot and short trail leading down to Sandcut Beach, surely one of the most interesting because of its two waterfalls that drop from an overhanging sandstone lip right onto the beach. Rope swings above the freshwater pools add to the fun. You can walk from here along the shore all the way to Jordan River, about four kilometres.

Jordan River, at the mouth of the stream that provides hydro power for most of southern Vancouver Island from an upriver reservoir, is an old logging community that has seen livelier times. Its wide shingle beach is popular with surfers and there's a small campsite and picnic area on the spit just before the log bridge. Birdwatchers will want to stop here, particularly from October through December when black-legged kittiwakes frequent the tide-rip just off the river mouth. It's also a great place for sunsets.

China Beach Provincial Park is another good whale-watching and beach-combing spot (no camping here) and Mystic Beach west of San Simon Point is reached by a beautiful but steep woodland trail. From here the road travels quite high above the shore through forest in various stages of commercial life, from clearcut, through replanting, thinning and spacing. The road crosses Loss Creek on a huge log bridge and a small area here has been set aside as provincial park, undeveloped apart from a few primitive riverside trails. Climbing higher onto the shoulders of the mountains the road becomes steeper and more serpentine. Shortly beyond Loss Creek, watch for the sign for Som-

Opposite Page: Its graveyard smothered in erythroniums, the tiny church of St. Mary the Virgin at Metchosin is one of the prettiest sights of spring on Vancouver Island.

Right: Sunset from the spit at Jordan River.

Below Left: Fishboats in Sooke Harbour.

Below Right: The swing above the freshwater pools on Sandcut Beach.

brio Beach, with its small cave and waterfall, reached by a steep long trail. Local Indians believed the Sombrio area to be the warmest on the island, and came here for cures.

Beyond Sombrio Beach, the road heads away from the shore, angling around to reach the head of a deep U-shaped bay. The Spanish explorer Quimper named this natural harbour Puerto de San Juan, anchored his ships and ran a mule train up to the headwaters of the river where the sailors searched for gold. In 1859 Hugh McKay of Sooke investigated the Spanish diggings and found two other men already working there. Gold was discovered, but only in small amounts, never enough to cause a stampede. The settlement of Port Renfrew (first known as San Juan) today is chiefly a centre for logging and commercial fishing. Our country road ends here, for Port Renfrew is a worthy destination—leaving several options open for consideration.

For instance, it is well worth a side trip into the forests to see the world's largest Douglas fir. As you near Port Renfrew, the road makes a fairly sharp bend south and a logging road, signposted Red Creek Mainline, comes in from the north. Up this road, which runs straight and level on the bed of a former logging railway up the San Juan Valley, lies the Red Creek Fir, almost a thousand years old and 74 metres tall. Park at a Y-junction just about 14.5 kilometres from the highway and follow the right hand track up the hill past the Three Guardsmen (three giant cedars) and on to the foot of the huge Douglas fir, identified, if there is any doubt, by a sign at its base giving all the statistics.

From the Red Creek Mainline the highway continues straight into town, ending at the government wharf and the old hotel. A left turn before the wharf, Cerantes Road, winds down to the headland to Botanical Beach, a spectacular area of sandstone ledges worn by the sea into tide pools of all sizes and teeming with sea life, a marine biologist's paradise best explored at low tide. Site of the world's first marine research station around the turn of the century and a gun emplacement during the Second World War, the beach today is part of a wilderness provincial park and nature reserve, a beautiful spot indeed. However, the road is long, extremely rough and, in the spring of 1991, impassable because of a washed out bridge. Four-wheelers may be able to negotiate the road if the bridge is repaired but otherwise be prepared for a hike. Undoubtedly, now that the area is an official park, access and facilities here will be improved.

A right turn off the highway just before the wharf takes you into the village itself with its neat houses strung along the bay and a very long wooden bridge over the river mouth. Several of the homes provide overnight accommodation for hikers beginning or ending the West Coast Trail. Two big rivers flow into the sea at the square head of Port San Juan: the San Juan itself, on the south and the Gordon River on the north. The West Coast Trail begins on the far side of the Gordon and hikers must arrange to be ferried across its wide mouth to the trailhead. Fishing here is excellent—chinooks, halibut and coho, smelts off the long sandy beach in summer, and steelhead and rainbows in the lakes and rivers.

An easy backroad leads up the San Juan River and this used to be a good way back to the east coast at Shawnigan Lake. But in 1987 the Williams Creek bridge (known familiarly as the Bedsprings Bridge because of its amazingly long and sagging span) about 45 kilometres along was closed as unsafe and not replaced, effectively severing this useful road connection. Even so, the road as far as Bedsprings is worth exploring if only because of the river, which offers innumerable excuses for picnics and fishing stops, and several impressive old logging bridges.

At Fairy Lake, much closer to town, there's a great little forestry campsite with beaches and a float for swimming. Canoeists may want to launch in the lake and navigate the short exit stream down to the river, but remember that the river here is tidal and currents can be tricky.

The main public exit route from Port Renfrew takes off north from the Harris Creek junction about 13 kilometres up the San Juan River. It's a mainline logging road that goes north all the way to Cowichan Lake, making possible a long loop tour. Tiny Lizard Lake, just past the intersection, provides campsites, a diving platform on a float and good fishing. But the lake is noteworthy for another reason: it is full of salamanders. Twenty kilometres along, a signpost directs travellers to the site of the former Harris Creek logging camp where a forest company sign provides statistics on another giant tree, a Sitka spruce. (The San Juan valley was famous for spruce back in the days when airplanes were made of the light but strong wood.) But alas: how have the mighty fallen! This giant is merely the butt end of a log. The way to Cowichan Lake is long, rough and in summer, dusty. Unless you are dead set on making a loop tour, it might be as well to turn around and head back along the West Coast Road, sampling the beaches as you go.

SAGEBRUSH SOLITUDES

For a good taste of Okanagan backcountry, for excellent birding, some geology, history and even astronomy, there is no better place than the high pocket of land wedged between the towns of Keremeos, Oliver and Okanagan Falls. Here, in an arid inner sanctum, the White Lake Dominion Radio Astrophysical Observatory fishes the sky for radio signals from outer space. Development round about has been restricted so that the giant scanners can operate without radio interference and this fact alone has kept the area lovely and lonely, a wild, uninterrupted stretch of sagebrush uplands.

It is day-trip country: the area is small and self-contained and can be infiltrated on a spider's web of roads which start from four different points. One through-route enters at the orchard town of Oliver and exits north of Okanagan Falls on the way to Penticton. At the traffic lights in downtown Oliver take the Fairview road which leads west through residential streets onto orchard benches, then higher still onto a sagebrush-covered flat high above the valley. This is the site of Fairview, the Okanagan's own goldrush town which shone brightly around the turn of the century and vanished with hardly a trace. A government stop of interest plaque, an old city street plan and a cross indicating the site of the 1889 presbyterian church are the only markers. For years the old town jail, a tiny log building, stood here at the mercy of vandals but it has been removed to the Oliver museum for safekeeping.

It was high-grade lode gold in the hills behind Fairview that gave impetus to the town in 1887 when the famous Stemwinder deposits were staked. A rush to the area followed and soon there were other mines: Morning Star, Tin Horn, Wildhorse, Smuggler, Brown Bear and Rattler, several with their own mills, and the mining camp in the tight little valley of Reed Creek sprawled out onto the flats below to become the leading town in the South Okanagan. Its population topped 5,000. It had everything necessary for urban life: stores and livery stables, a Chinese laundry, blacksmith's shop, doctor's office, school, two churches, government offices, jailhouse and sundry private residences. And its six hotels included the Fairview, a three-storey palace with an elegant gothic tower which prompted its nickname of "The Big Tepee".

Fairview survived a typhoid epidemic and a disastrous fire which levelled the Big Tepee in 1902, but it could not survive the death of the mines. The mining companies soon realized that while the gold deposits were rich, they occurred only in small isolated pockets and were costly to reach; one by one they pulled up stakes and moved out. By 1910, Fairview was finished and the townsfolk moved away. But the treasures of Fairview were not yet exhausted. In the late 1960s souvenir hunters identified the site of the Big Tepee and dug in the earth where the hotel had stood. They hit pay dirt. Out of the rubble came gold and silver coins, gold and diamond rings, gold watch chains and silver spoons, items lost when guests fled for their lives in the great fire.

Deserted buildings in the dry Okanagan air don't rot, but they burn like kindling. A few of the Fairview homes were broken up for lumber or moved away, several to the new settlement of Oliver below, and the rest went up in flames. The only gold these days is in the sunflowers blazing on the hills near the cemetery in May and in the golden notes of nesting meadowlarks.

To see some of the mining relics continue

Left: White Lake sits in the hollow of a great sagebrush bowl. In spring, look for opuntia cactus and blue mertensia.

Below Left: Simple cross marks the location of the presbyterian church in Fairview, the empty site of a goldmining town above Oliver.

Above Right: A country road skirts the edges of the empty sagebrush expanse around White Lake.

Right: The main radio telescope at the Dominion Astrophysical Observatory scans the sky for messages from outer space.

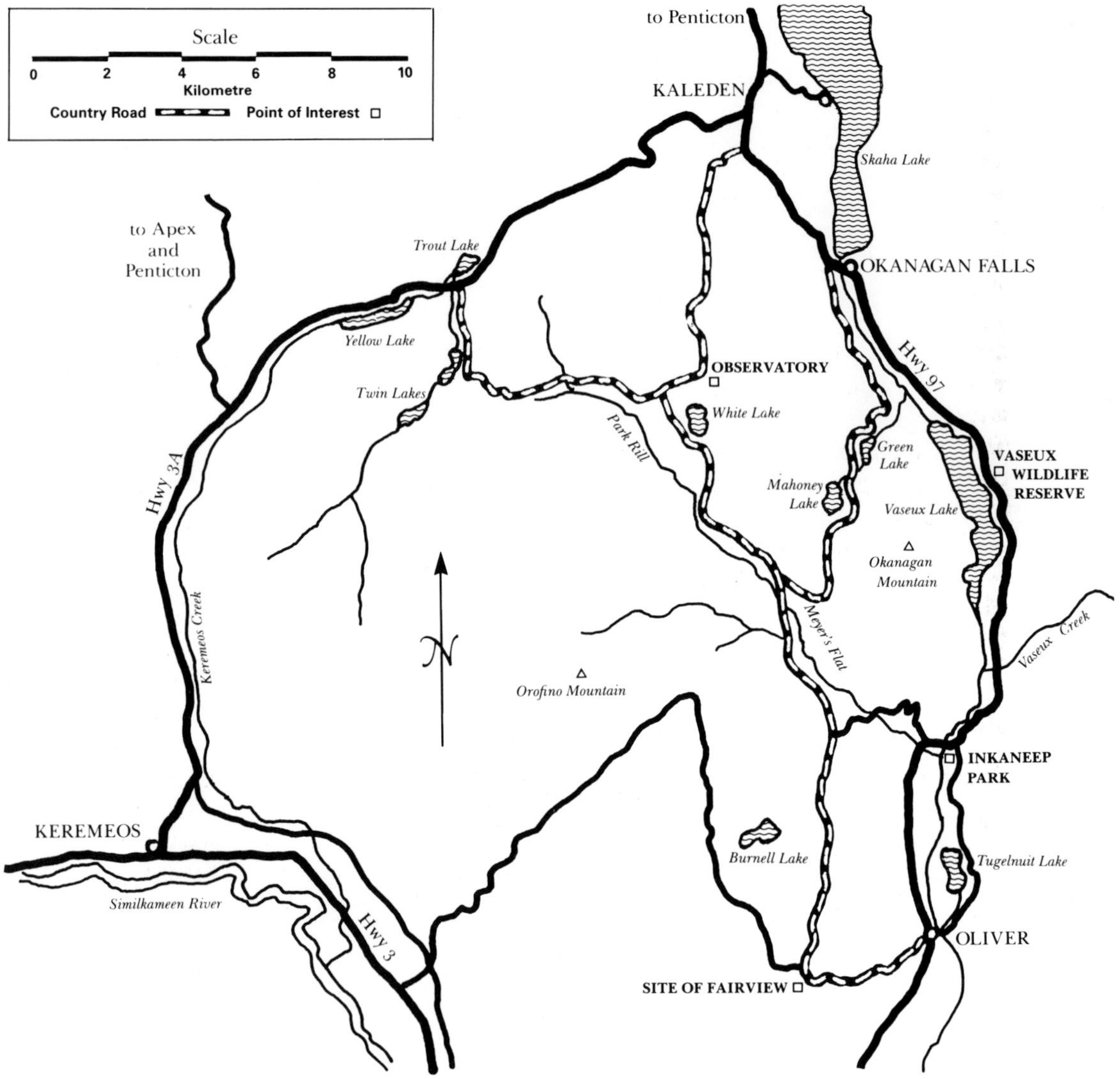

straight along the road that follows the creek into the forested gulch, site of the earliest Fairview camp. Here were the mines and the stampmills, the rowdiest of the miner's saloons and boarding houses. Now there is little to see: a few foundations, piles of rocks and a few old tunnels, but the road itself is worth a drive. It continues up the creek onto the shoulder of Orofino Mountain then angles around southwest to follow Blind Creek down to the Similkameen Valley east of Keremeos. The road is closed in winter and not recommended for vehicles other than cars and pick-up trucks.

To reach White Lake, turn off the Fairview Road by the old townsite and take the signposted road north. This snakes along a narrow valley, beaded with ponds and fringed with ponderosa pines. Five kilometres along, a turning leads left to Burnell Lake, a good fishing spot, while the road that comes in from the east a few kilometres farther on leads back down to Highway 97 near Inkaneep Provincial Park. Historians believe that the original fur-brigade route north up the Okanagan Valley to Fort Kamloops left the main valley here to seek better grazing for the horses. For the rest of the way, our country route will follow the general direction of the historic trail. Meyers Flats, the meadows which begin just north of the junction, may have been one of the brigade campsites.

Today, this area is the best place in the province for birders to see poor-wills. Members of the nightjar family, they are easily seen on summer evenings crouching beside the road picking up the insects which hover over the warm asphalt. Wait until almost dark and drive very slowly; your headlights may pick up a pair of ruby eyes on the road ahead. The birds will often allow you to approach quite close before fluttering off, like huge grey moths. Their "poor will" cry is unmistakable.

At the top end of Meyers Flats the road forks; the right branch, signposted Green Lake, leads along a little-travelled route to Okanagan Falls, passing two bird-rich lakes, Mahoney and Green. Look along here for nesting redheads, goldeneyes, spotted sandpipers and the rare white-headed woodpecker. Then the road descends swiftly through vineyards down to the Okanagan Valley at the north end of Vaseux Lake wildlife reserve, probably the very best birding spot in the Okanagan, with trumpeter swans, yellow-breasted chats, lazuli buntings, pygmy nuthatches, white-throated swifts, and rock wrens. The dykes here provide foot passage but there is better access from Highway 97, on the east side of the lake. Once down at valley level, the road follows the river to Okanagan Falls. For bird enthusiasts, this is definitely a road to explore.

Back to our route, bear left at the Green Lake junction and drive through the tight little valley of Park Rill, a small, meandering creek which keeps the ranch fields green, providing good cover for California quail. The road climbs out of the valley by some steep volcanic bluffs and rounds a corner by Dry Lake, in summer merely an alkaline patch of cracked earth. The cliffs behind are worth study, both for their craggy castle formations and for possible sightings of rock wrens and swifts. This is the lip of the White Lake basin, an expansive area of undulating sagebrush with a huge population of singing meadowlarks and lots of spring flowers. Look for early pink phlox, mountain bluebells, yellow fritillary, blue phacelia, bitterroot and cactus flowers.

The road climbs higher into the basin where White Lake sits like milk in a teacup. The lake itself is alkaline: it is usually thickly rimmed with white and in summer might be dried up entirely. But it still provides good birding. There are often several pairs of long-billed curlews nesting here as well as Grasshopper and Brewer's sparrows and the area is the best place in Canada to see sage thrashers. At the cattle guard a dirt track leads off towards a log corral and the east shore of the lake, a good observation spot away from the road.

When the fur-traders came this way, the flats were was richly clothed in bunchgrass and the first settlers grazed their cattle here. By 1923 Charles Camsell's geological survey showed that already the grass had been replaced by sage, a sign of overgrazing. He also recorded a post-office here and charted some surface coal deposits which had been discovered earlier and put to use by the blacksmith at Fairview. The coal was mined sporadically and in a small way until 1933.

The White Lake Observatory lies just over the rim of the basin and its great metal scanners and its gridwork of poles seem out of place on this lonely moorland. Follow the road around the basin slope and turn right at the major intersection. Birders should pause at the watertank just beyond and look for mountain bluebirds, Say's phoebes and lazuli buntings. Everyone must stop at the entrance to the observatory for the road in is closed to vehicles. Visitors must walk along the short road which leads alongside a line of radio telescopes and up to the main installation. There are explanation boards, recorded messages and a museum but guided tours of the facility are given only on Sunday afternoons in July and August.

From the observatory continue north along the route of the fur-traders, stopping after one kilometre to look for fossils in the shale beds on the road's eastern side, past tiny Prather Lake, where the brigade trail probably branched off, heading for the Marron Valley. The golf-course and artificial lake of St. Andrews residential complex spreads out to the west and the dry pine forests beyond are a good place to look for Townsend's solitaire. Highway 97 lies ahead, just seven kilometres from the observatory turning.

There is one other exit from White Lake to explore: the left turn from the observatory which continues west around the other rim of the sagebrush bowl past White Lake Ranch and down to Twin Lakes with its cluster of summer homes. This road will bring you out beside another golfcourse on Highway 3A north of Keremeos.

ALONG THE GOLDRUSH TRAIL

The landscape on the eastern side of B.C.'s Cariboo Plateau is very different from the dry open benches above the Fraser. Here, the country is closed in, densely carpeted with jack pine and spruce forest, a maze of creeks and lakes and wide rushing rivers, difficult even today for road builders to traverse. Lieutenant H. Spencer Palmer of the Royal Engineers, sent out from New Westminster in the 1860s to survey a wagon road to the goldfields through this obdurate country, reported on the state of the trails: "slippery, precipitous ascents and descents, fallen logs, overhanging branches, roots, rocks, swamps, turbid pools and miles of deep mud . . . dreaded alike by all classes of travellers". But travellers came anyway, thousands of them, whatever the season, whatever the hazards, because in the creeks lay gold.

Once the early Goldrush Trail left the Fraser, it ploughed its way northeast from the area of Williams Lake to the forks of the Quesnel River and up to Quesnel Lake; then it headed up the Cariboo River to Keithley Creek and over the Snowshoe Plateau to the great gold-bearing creeks of Antler and Williams. Ahead lay Barkerville, the greatest goldrush town of them all.

Gold was first found on the Horsefly River in June of 1859; in July it was also reported on the Quesnel River. All the miners from the played-out bars along the Fraser rushed upstream and took to the hills, looking for the mother lode. Instant towns sprang up wherever the miners camped. Quesnel Forks at the confluence of the Quesnel and Cariboo Rivers was the first, built where a ferry, then a toll bridge carried traffic across the river. Hard on its heels came Keithley, followed by Antler, Van Winkle, Richfield, Camerontown and finally, Barkerville, in 1864. It is interesting that of all of these, only the first and last have survived, one in lonely decay, the other as a reconstructed historic park.

To retrace the first route to the Cariboo mines, take the country road which branches east from 150 Mile House, signposted to Likely and Horsefly. The route is mostly paved, straightened and smoothed out by modern engineering; the horrors of the original trail are no more. Today you can drive quickly and pleasantly to some of the old and interesting places: to the huge hole in the ground that is or was the Bullion mine, to the old towns of Likely and Horsefly and, best of all, to the lovely ghost of Quesnel Forks.

The first site to visit is Crosina's Store at the old 153-Mile House, along a cut-off section of the wagon road three kilometres from the highway junction. Why did the wagon road come this way instead of taking the easier route, already surveyed, along the shore of Williams Lake then north up the Fraser? It seems that the road contractor, J.B. Wright, dependent on funds shipped out from Victoria, found himself temporarily short of the cash needed to meet the payroll. Work stopped at 140-Mile while he appealed to the owner of the roadhouse at William's Lake (the site of today's town) for a loan. This was refused. Insulted, he turned to the more accommodating owners of property along the trail at 150-Mile who were glad to help, provided the road came their way. Thus, the wagon road and all the traffic on it turned away from the river, bypassing the roadhouse in Williams Lake and bringing prosperity instead to 150-Mile (and coincidentally, to a roadhouse on Deep Creek in which Wright was a partner.) At 153-Mile House along the new wagon road, Alice Crosina ran the ranch store all her life, from girlhood until her death in 1963. Now part of the Patenaude Ranch, the faded red and white log store is closed now but it's said to be still stocked with goods, just the way Miss Crosina left it. Perhaps one day it will be a museum. It's private property, so ask permission at the house if you plan to poke around.

Two kilometres beyond Crosina's, the road forks, the left branch leading to Likely, the one ahead to Horsefly. Turn left here and follow the route of the old trail and the wagon road for another two kilometres to the vanished site of 158-Mile, or Mountain House. Here the wagon road turned to follow Deep Creek, today's Hawks Creek, to the end of the road at Soda Creek on the Fraser. (In the early years the next leg of the journey to the mouth of the Quesnel River was by boat). Those seeking to retrace the wagon road route will want to turn here, but there is little to see. Frank Way's property at 164-Mile (and the roadhouse that Wright helped to establish) was returned to the Crown in 1899 and became part of the Deep Creek Indian reserve. The first trail to the Cariboo forges on for about 15 kilometres through spruce forest and past aspen-fringed Skulow Lake, then breaks out into rolling meadowland with old snake fences, barns and cabins. At 35 kilometres (from 150-Mile) there's the little community of Big Lake, with a ranch on the lake itself, a small store and a gas station. Nearby are several guest ranches, and a host of other smaller lakes. Fishing for rainbow trout is one of the attractions. From here the road crosses the hump of Limestone Mountain and descends into the Beaver Valley. Where the road curves around to cross the creek, a wide sideroad heads west for 39 kilometres to join Highway 97 at McLeese Lake.

The huddle of old log ranch buildings here marks the site of Beaver Lake House, one of the most famous of the stopping places on the trail. Established in 1861 by Peter Dunlevy who had made the first gold strike of the Cariboo on the Horsefly River, it later passed to Francois Guy. A miner, J.C. Bryant, praised Beaver Lake House in his journal of 1863. "The hotel is the best between Victoria and the Cariboo, indeed Victoria hotels could not compare with this one in the splendid meals given to the guests". He went on to describe a sumptuous dinner of baked meats, fresh vegetables, huge huckleberry pies and cream. In addition to the hotel, two stores were here, a gambling hall and a thriving market for pack animals. The original buildings have vanished, the site is now occupied by the Hamilton Ranch and the new road bypasses the old bridge across the creek.

The deep dandelion meadows here are stitched around the edges by a graceful log fence which borders the road on its journey up the hillside where a gravel sideroad leads southeast through the Beaver Valley to Horsefly (our return route). The Likely road climbs high into the forests of the plateau, passing the University of B. C. Research Forest at Gavin Lake and a resort on Moorehead Lake. This lake is a water storage reservoir formed when the creek was dammed in 1898 to provide water for huge hydraulicing operations at the Bullion mine in nearby Dancing Bill's Gulch. Dancing Bill, alias Thomas Latham struck gold on the Quesnel River late in 1859 but stayed only a while to glean the easy pickings. Twenty years later the claim was reworked by Chinese who dug into the river benches and discovered almost $1 million in gold on the old riverbed. They cleaned up in turn and went on their way.

In 1892, with Cariboo fever abated, J.B. Hobson formed a syndicate to extract gold from the gulch by hydraulicing. To obtain waterpower for this scheme, at the time the greatest hydraulic enterprise in the world, Hobson and his partners built nearly 35 kilometres of ditches to carry water down from Bootjack and Polley lakes and from the great reservoir behind Moorehead dam. The gravel banks of the old river benches were pressure sluiced with giant hoses and millions of dollars' worth of gold was recovered from the filtered sludge. Every year, Dancing Bill's Gulch became wider and deeper and soon more water was needed. Hobson began plans to divert water from Spanish Creek, 20 kilometres away but in 1906, with no word of explanation, his U.S. backers pulled out and all work on the Bullion mine was abandoned. Almost 30 years later the mine was reopened and worked for a further ten years. But since then, the gigantic hole in the ground has been left alone.

Ten kilometres beyond Moorehead, near the site of the turn-of-the-century town of Hydraulic, the gold miners' trail turned left towards the bridge over the Quesnel River. Today a rough road signposted to the Bullion Pit, it is worth the drive, if only to stand on the lip of the enormous man-made crater, three kilometres long and a hundred metres deep, to survey the damage that water, and man, has inflicted. Little else remains.

The bridge over the river here has long since vanished. To reach Quesnel Forks today you must first go to Likely, passing the Quesnel River Salmon Hatchery en route. A narrow wooden bridge crosses the river at Likely on the same spot where in 1897 Joseph Hunter and a crew of 500 men built a dam across the river to hold back the waters while they took out the gold in the river channel. The

Left: On the Horsefly Road in spring the fields are brilliant with wildflowers, including dense stands of orange agerosis.

Below and Top Right: Quesnel Forks, probably the oldest and certainly the loveliest ghost town of the Cariboo gold rush.

Right: in the Quesnel Forks cemetery.

Bottom Right: On the outskirts of Horsefly.

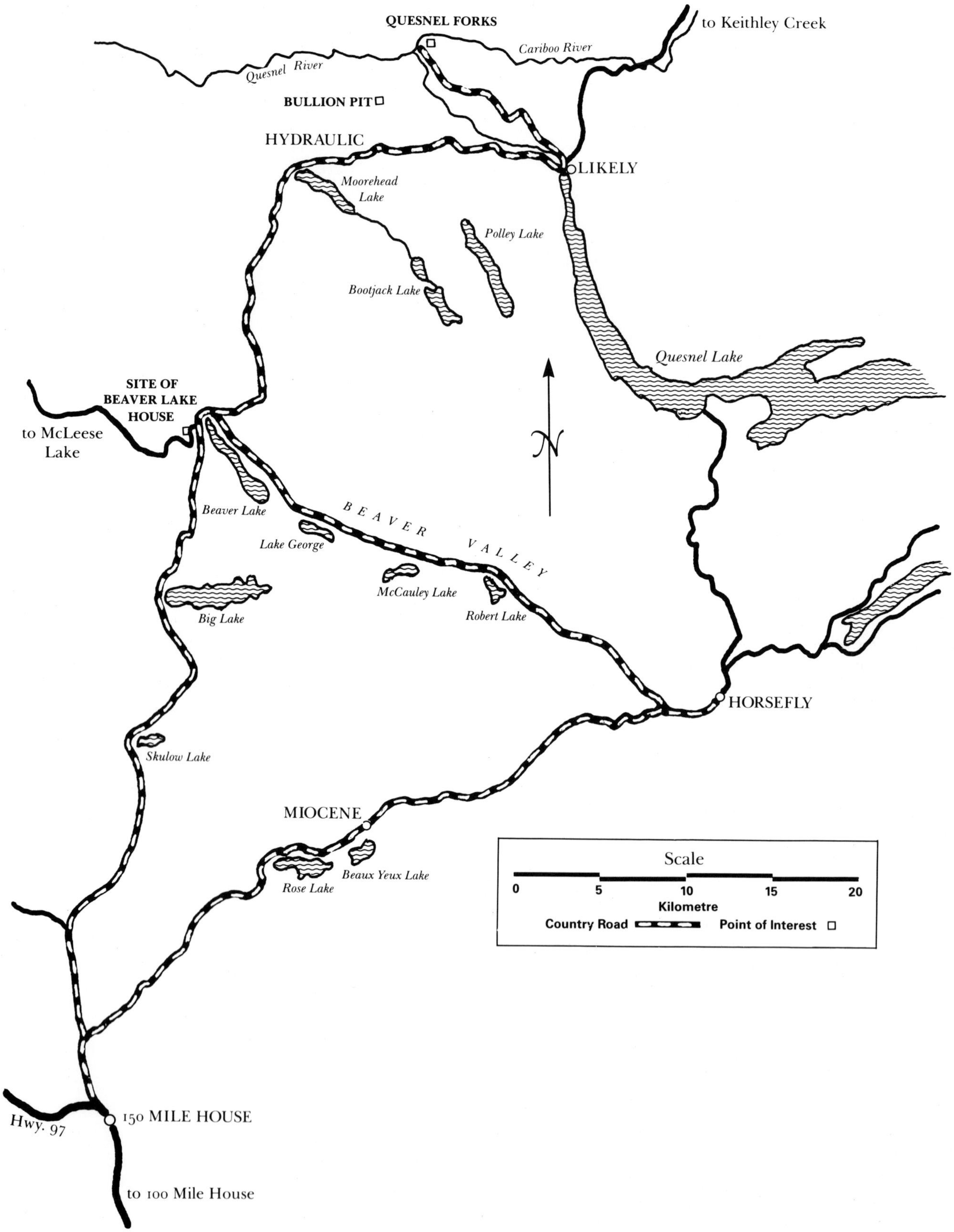
QUESNEL FORKS
to Keithley Creek
Cariboo River
Quesnel River
BULLION PIT
HYDRAULIC
LIKELY
Moorehead Lake
Polley Lake
Bootjack Lake
Quesnel Lake
SITE OF BEAVER LAKE HOUSE
to McLeese Lake
Beaver Lake
BEAVER VALLEY
Lake George
Big Lake
McCauley Lake
Robert Lake
HORSEFLY
Skulow Lake
MIOCENE
Rose Lake
Beaux Yeux Lake
Scale
0 5 10 15 20
Kilometre
Country Road
Point of Interest
Hwy. 97
150 MILE HOUSE
to 100 Mile House

settlement that grew up here was first known as Quesnel Dam, then renamed after John "Plato" Likely who worked claims in a nearby gulch. John earned his nickname because he was a great admirer of Plato and Socrates and would talk philosophy for hours. Today, a hotel, cafe, store, gas station and other tourist facilities are strung out along the main riverside street.

Instead of turning in to Likely centre, take the road which leads up behind it and watch for a turning signposted for Quesnel Forks. The 12 kilometres of narrow, rough road lead up and over a forested ridge, cutting off a curve in the river, and the climb down to the river again is steep: once again the route of the Goldrush Trail. Quesnel Forks lies in the arms of the Quesnel and Cariboo Rivers, the latter originally known as the North Fork. Surveyed in 1861 by the Royal Engineers, the townsite was briefly the largest settlement on the B.C. mainland. Here on the river bank were 20 houses, a dozen stores, saloons, a Chinese joss house, cabins and a log government building with two jail cells. As the main supply centre for all the mines in the area it flourished and grew—and would probably have continued to grow if the wagon road had come this way to Barkerville. But the topography proved too difficult. Instead the route of choice went first from Soda Creek to Quesnel Mouth (today's Quesnel) by steamer, then across via Cottonwood and Barkerville, a route longer by nearly 60 kilometres than the old trail through Quesnel Forks.

This new road brought an end to the fortunes of the Forks. After only five years of glory, its inhabitants moved away. Later the townsite was adopted by the local Chinese community who continued to work the river bars for gold, but they left too. And Quesnel Forks finally became a ghost town, though it has never been quite deserted, for oldtimers live here still. Fifteen or so of the old log buildings remain on this quiet river bench under the cottonwood trees. They were sturdily built of massive logs and will last longer yet, given a chance. Meanwhile, every spring more of the town is undercut by the river; roofs collapse and vandals attack. The site is still a beautiful one, with strong ties to B.C.'s turbulent history, and it deserves preservation. A forest service campsite now occupies the townsite. And in the scattered graveyard only a few headstones remain, tangled in salmonberry.

Return to Likely the way you came and drive back along the road until you come to Beaver Lake. Take the Horsefly road which follows Beaver Creek southeast through idyllic Beaver Valley with its string of little marshy lakes and old homesteads. Beaver Creek Ranch has a display of antlers; Robert Lake some beautiful yellow lilies and a Forest Service recreation site. And then there's the B S Ranch—no kidding!

It's 34 kilometres to the village of Horsefly which is on the river but not the lake of the same name. It was on the Horsefly River that Peter Dunlevy found the first gold in the Cariboo in 1859 and the settlement was originally called Harper's after the first homesteaders, the brothers who went on to found the Gang Ranch. Today the village is quiet and picturesque, a well-equipped tourist centre for big-game hunting and fishing. On the lake, about 13 kilometres from the village, is Horsefly Lake Provincial Park, a good place to camp or launch a boat. There's a beach for swimming.

From Horsefly, undoubtedly named for the insects that plague all campers, you can return to 150-Mile House along 50 kilometres of paved highway that passes alternately through forests and farm clearings. In a wet spring the fields and ditches are thick with wildflowers: shiny clouds of buttercups, drifts of tiger lilies, red columbine, lupines and Indian paintbrush. This part of B.C. is in the Interior wet belt; the forests are mostly cedar and hemlock, jungled with skunk cabbage and devil's club and the flowers are very different from those on the dry Fraser benches. Sixteen kilometres before the Likely junction, you will pass a small community with the intriguing name of Miocene. Can it really be that old?

THE HOOFBEATS OF HISTORY

There are not many authentic traces left of the old Cariboo Wagon Road. The building of the highway and its constant improvement have obliterated most of it; settlements have faded away and most of the historic landmarks are gone, including all but three of the colourful inns or roadhouses. Travellers who drive Highway 97 today eager for traces of history on their way north to Barkerville may be disappointed. But if you know where to look, sections of the original road can still be found, abandoned when the highway cut off a corner or followed a different route. Here the hoofbeats of history still echo, for those who care to hear.

This country road ends at one of the original roadhouses, still beautifully intact, that sits on a well-preserved 16-kilometre stretch of the wagon road. No longer a public thoroughfare, this old and stony track provides access through an Indian reserve and to ranches along the Bonaparte River, and while it is possible to drive along it, the route deserves a slower and more respectful approach. A walk along this road in the footsteps of the thousands of miners who tramped this way will be a good introduction to the goldrush experience—and a splendid climax to a day of backcountry explorations.

The 60-kilometre route begins by turning off the Trans Canada Highway south of Ashcroft, climbs high over the Cornwall Hills then follows Hat Creek down to the roadhouse and Highway 97 north of Cache Creek, a country road guaranteed to beat both the heat and the congestion of the summer highways. Travellers coming north along the Trans Canada Highway should look for a left turning just beyond the Red Hill rest stop, about 38 kilometres north of Spences Bridge. Marked for Hat Creek, the road passes the corrals of a large cattle feedlot. But don't start yet.

Ten kilometres up the highway lies Ashcroft Manor, another of the authentic Cariboo Roadhouses, and a visit here is thoroughly recommended, if only for the food. Built in 1862 by brothers Henry and Clement Cornwall, this historic establishment has been serving the public almost continuously now for 130 years. The brothers left their village of Ashcroft in Gloucestershire, England, to join the gold rush but became ranchers instead, pre-empting land and putting down roots on the deep bunchgrass of the Thompson River flats that promised a future more certain than gold. In 1859 they built a small cabin and drove in cattle from Idaho. They called their ranch Ashcroft Manor after their English home. When the wagon road passed through their land in 1862 the brothers built a stopping place at the 104-Mile post (measured from Yale), and this, too, was known as Ashcroft. The original structure, since enlarged and modified, can still be seen.

The Cornwall boys, unlike many of the newcomers to B.C. at that time, had education and money. Clement had a Cambridge arts degree and had been called to the Temple Bar in London as a barrister. When the brothers married and settled down they tried to make Ashcroft as much like home as possible. They built an Anglican church with a steeple and eight high-backed pews. They imported English nannies for their children, kept up the customs of English tea and garden parties,

Left and Below: Hat Creek House, one of the few remaining roadhouses along the Cariboo Wagon Road.

Right: Indian paintbrush, familiar roadside flame.

held horse races on nearby Cornwall Flats and even established the Ashcroft Hunt. Over the sagebrush and prickly pear, over the waving bunchgrass went the hunters, dressed out in natty scarlet, with hunting horns and a pack of hounds imported from England. The fact that there were no foxes to hunt did not bother them: they went after coyotes instead. Clement Cornwall went on to become an MLA, a senator, a judge and in 1881 Lieutenant-Governor of B.C.

This little bit of English high society, the social hub of the area, flourished in the colonial wilderness in the years when its only link with civilization was the Cariboo Road. The ranch supplied the mining camps with beef, sawn lumber and later, with milled flour from wheat grown on the arid benches. But when the Canadian Pacific Railway built through the Thompson Valley in the 1880s, the wagon road declined and the focus of settlement shifted to Ashcroft Station down by the river. The roadhouse, however, remained open for many years. Today the old house itself with its long shady verandah has become shops selling antiques, memorabilia, B.C. crafts and tourist souvenirs. And behind the house a newly-built teahouse keeps up the Ashcroft tradition of hospitality, serving some of the best food in the Cariboo, including huge pots of tea and home baking in an English-style dining room. On the Indian reserve beside the Ashcroft road, St. John's Church, built in the Manor's heyday, still displays its sturdy hand-hewn log walls, neatly dovetailed at the corners, and its diminutive steeple.

From Ashcroft Manor, return south down the highway and take the Hat Creek road which follows Oregon Jack Creek up into the hills. Oregon Jack was the nickname of John Dowling from Oregon who ran a stopping place nearby. The road climbs steeply through sagebrush, then dives into welcome forest shade, cutting back to follow the creek valley past several small ranches. At 13.5 kilometres from the highway, the road splits: ahead up Three Sisters Creek lies a steep mountain track leading to the Cornwall Forestry Lookout which sits at 2,230 metres elevation on the summit of the ridge. Unless it's early spring or the road is wet, two-wheel drive family cars can make this trip reasonably comfortably, but if you have any doubts, then park the car and walk. It will be a nine-kilometre hike each way, so go prepared with water and a snack. The alpine meadows on the open slopes below the lookout are brilliant in July with wildflowers and the view is magnificent. On a clear day you can see south to Mount Baker, east to the Rockies and north to Mount Waddington.

Down from the lookout, turn right and continue past the Forest Service Three Sisters Recreation Site and continue up Oregon Jack valley, a valley that quickly becomes very much a box canyon, headed by steep, colourful cliffs and floored by deep green meadows. The road climbs above the canyon, keeping in the shade of the Douglas fir forest, up and over the low pass at a cattleguard. From now on, it's downhill past some interesting rock outcrops of a brilliant orange-ochre into a tight little valley where beaver dams have created a series of marshy ponds. The road is narrow here, in places one-lane only, and fringed with trembling aspens whose fallen leaves in autumn turn the track into a golden road. Langley Lake, farther along, marks the beginning of the hayfields and soon the valley widens out into the larger landscape of Hat Creek. At 23 kilometres from the highway, turn right at the junction by a log barn and corrals and head east. (If you look back, you will see a sign warning that the road you have just driven is not suitable for passenger cars when wet or frosty.)

The Hat Creek Valley is a beautiful one with wide-reaching horizons of forested blue rising above the rich green of irrigated ranchlands. Not so long ago the valley, underlain by huge deposits of lignite coal, was scheduled to become the site of a vast open-pit mine, the products of which would be used to fuel a huge electric power plant. Environmentalists fought the scheme because of potential air and water pollution; ranchers because it would mean the destruction of valuable farmland, land that has been in the same families for generations. For the moment, B.C. Hydro has dropped the scheme; the valley has won a reprieve from what would have been a death sentence in terms of scenery.

The road leads along the southern edge of the valley past a succession of old ranches. One of the oldest belongs to the Parke family, founded by Philip Parke who came to Canada from Ireland in 1862, lured by prospects of gold. The Parkes' first ranch was on the Bonaparte River but they used the land up the Hat as summer meadows where they cut natural hay. The first cabin on the Hat Creek property dates from 1912. Today the ranchhouse with its gables and verandahs and soft green roof (about two kilometres from the junction) is in disrepair but nearby are sturdy corrals and spanking new barns and sheds for the new Parke enterprise, the raising of European fallow deer. If you stop and scan the valley behind the very high wire fences (built to keep the fallow deer in and local deer and predators out) you can see the animals,

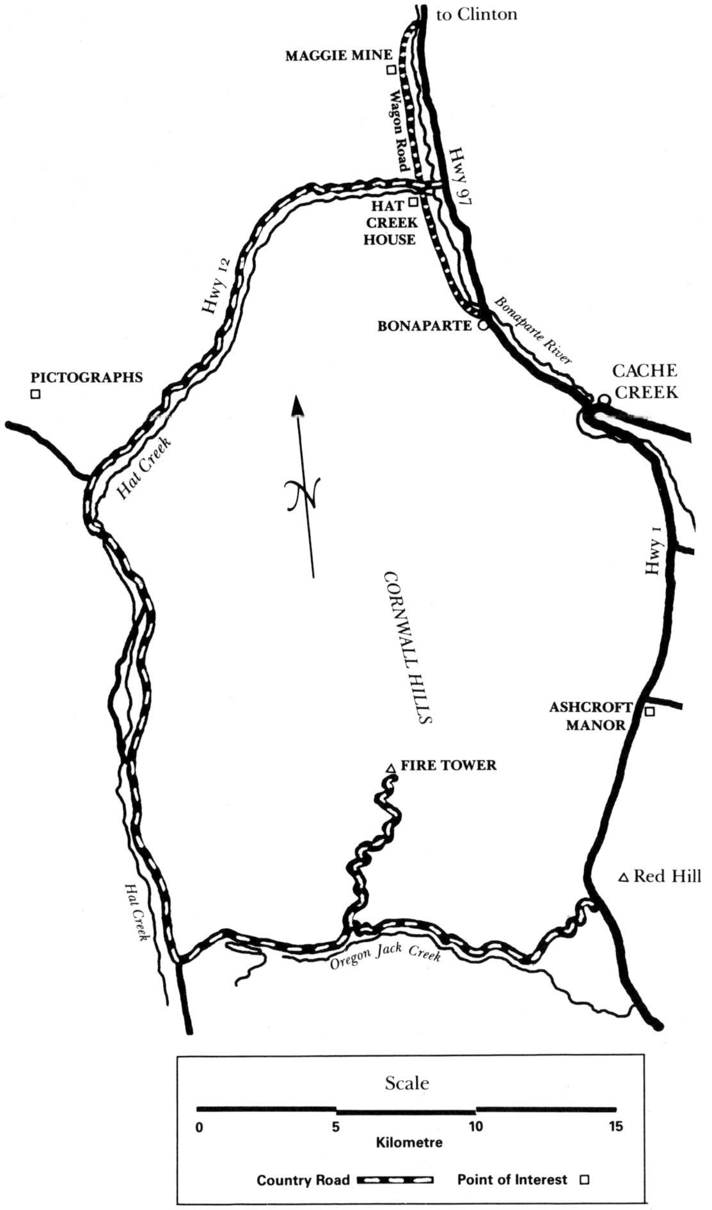

hundreds of them, usually where the meadows meet the trees. A couple which are farm pets can often be seen lolling about behind the ranchhouse.

Past the Parke ranch is Upper Hat Creek Ranch with an old log house, barns and corrals. A few alkaline lakes beside the road are surrounded by stones furred with bright orange lichen. You can count on seeing killdeer nesting here and look for horned larks and kestrels perching on roadside poles. In the open pine woods to the south, May brings great clumps of balsamroot sunflowers The road plunges on, past some sod-roof buildings beside a cattleguard and across Hat Creek beside an old irrigation flume. Then it meets Highway 12 up from Lillooet by way of Pavilion and Marble Canyon and our route turns right (east) to follow Hat Creek to its confluence with the Bonaparte River.

But first, if you are interested in Indian pictographs, there are some splendid panels on creamy-coloured limestone cliffs a few kilometres west along the road. To find them, drive a little over three kilometres towards Pavilion and follow a sketchy trail which starts up a steep rocky gulley. When you reach the cliffs, about a kilometre from the road, look for a small high cave: the pictographs are below, painted in red on four separate panels stretching around the hillside for 50 metres.

Highway 12 running east is pleasant enough, but the highlight of the day lies just off the road about 20 kilometres ahead: Hat Creek House, a long building with a second-storey balcony forming a porch over the roadside facade, and with a surrounding cluster of old farm buildings. The loveliest of the remaining roadhouses, it is in singularly good repair. Now in the hands of the B.C. Heritage Trust and open to the public, its future is assured.

The first to settle on the creek was Donald McLean who retired here after many years as chief trader at the Hudson's Bay Company Kamloops post. McLean and his family squatted on the land in 1860 and started what was variously called McLean's, McLean's Station or McLean's Restaurant, but the first crown grant was obtained by William Cargile of Dog Creek who listed himself as "farmer and inn-keeper." The property was later owned by Steve Tingley, the crack whip of the B.C. Express Company, known as the BX, which operated the stage line between Yale and Soda Creek. The exact age of the present roadhouse is not known but it is believed to date from the 1880s and some of the surrounding buildings may go back to the 1860s. One could very well be the Hudson's Bay Company depot known to be on the site. A small log cabin beside the roadhouse is thought to be the original McLean home. Donald McLean, killed in 1864 by Indians after the Chilcotin Massacre, was the father of four sons, three of whom achieved notoriety as the "Wild McLean Boys" who murdered a constable near Kamloops in 1879.

Running in front of the Hat Creek Roadhouse is the original stretch of the old Cariboo Wagon Road, abandoned when the highway relocated on the east side of the Bonaparte valley. This winds south along the sagebrush slopes for 5.5 kilometres back to Highway 97 at the Bonaparte Indian Reserve north of Cache Creek. Here is St. Louis Church, built in 1894 of logs now covered with siding and with an interesting octagonal steeple. Across the highway the cemetery gates, a curving

Below: The flame-coloured outcrops at the Maggie Mine site contrast the rich greens of the Bonaparte Valley. Between the mine and the valley runs a scenic stretch of the original Cariboo Wagon Road, a great walk from Hat Creek House.

Below Left: Along the cross-over road from upper Hat Creek to Oregon Jack Creek; penstemon brightens the way.

Below Right: In April, balsamroot sunflowers emblazon the open woods that edge Hat Creek Valley.

Left: Peigan encampment at the Head-Smashed-In Pow-wow.

Below: The long and winding road through the grassy eastern slopes of the Porcupine Hills.

Right: At the foot of the Porcupine Hills and cradled in fall foliage, Alberta ranch is overlooked by the stern rock ridge of the Livingstone Range.

Below Left: The road through the Porcupines, looking west to the Rockies.

Below Right: Specially painted Peigan tipi was a gift to the Head-Smashed-In museum.

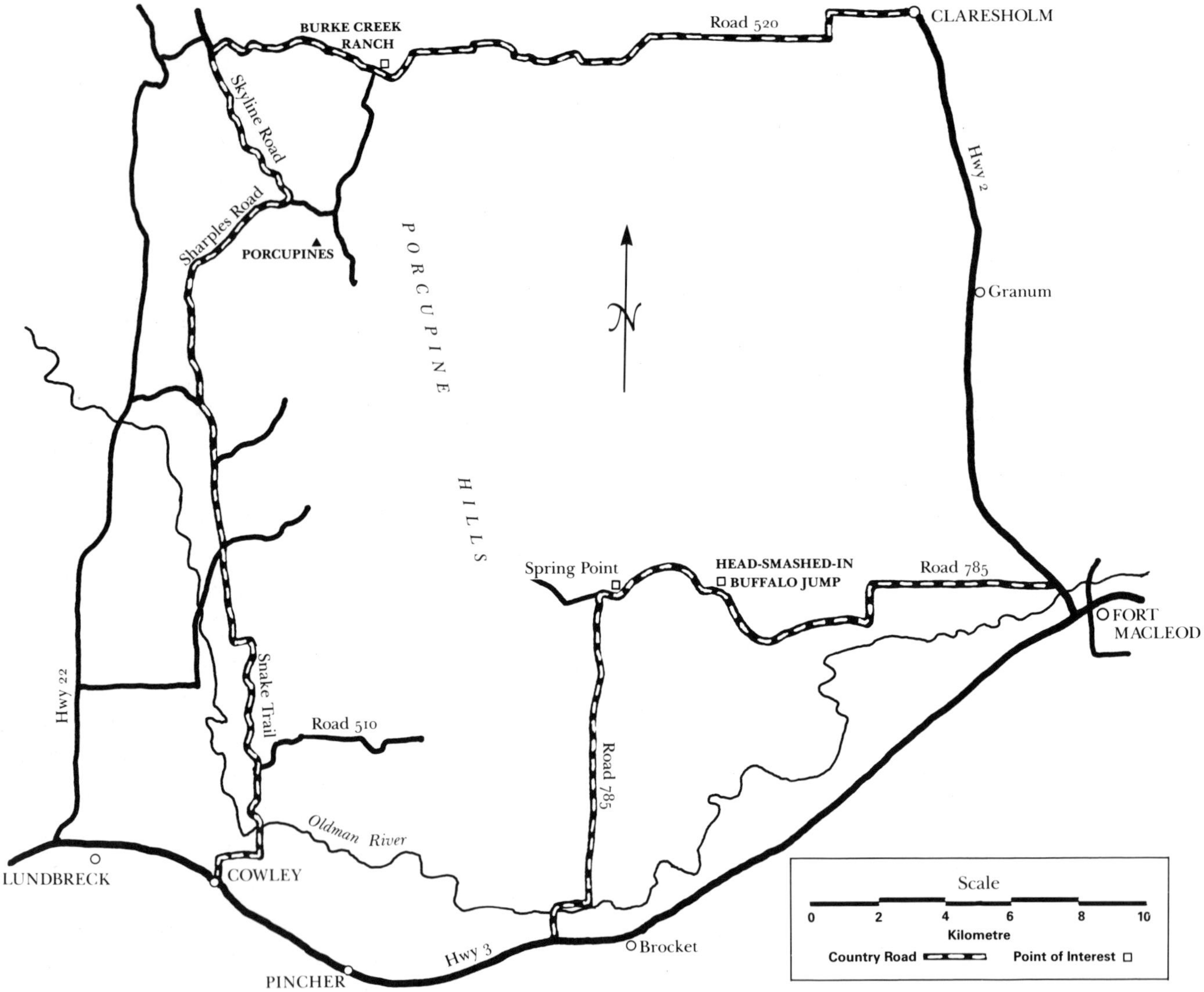

bridge and across to Highway 22.)

Sinuous both horizontally and vertically, the Snake Trail keeps to the edge of the hills high above the river valley. When we last drove this road the controversial dam across the river was under construction. This dam will impound the waters of the Oldman and flood much of the low-lying farmland, most of the pioneer ranches and many prehistoric Indian sites. But the old log barns and homesteads along the Snake Trail are high enough on the Porcupines' shoulders to escape the rising waters. Drive slowly along this road, enjoying its country curves, the sweep of the valley below, the farm fields, sometimes cultivated in strips, like a patchwork quilt, the rolling hills behind and the distant view of the Rockies to the southwest. In places, the ridges east of the road are knobby with sandstone outcrops made picture perfect by wind-swept evergreens and tassels of juniper. At about 90 kilometres the Snake Trail meets Secondary Road 510 which leads down to cross the Oldman River on the Blue Bridge, close to the dam construction site. And from the bridge it's just a short hop into the small community of Cowley, on Highway 3.

Topographic maps (and even recent government highway maps) show Road 510, signposted to Upper and Lower Tennessee, striking off to the east around the hills towards our destination. But this road, though the first few kilometres are easy to follow and satisfyingly scenic, soon degenerates into a confusion of junctions and sideroads, all of similar size and quality, so that finding the main route becomes a matter of guesswork. Try this connector, if you like, for it seems to be an interesting shortcut, but we don't recommend it.

When you hit Highway 3, turn east and drive through the community of Pincher Station and on towards Brocket. About six kilometres past Brocket, turn north along Secondary Road 785 which heads straight back towards the dark spiky humps of the Porcupines. This road is easy to follow: it is well signposted to Head-Smashed-in Buffalo Jump, one of Alberta's most famous archaeological sites and a UNESCO World Heritage Site. The road passes Springhouse Hutterite Community, makes a sharp east turn at the Springhouse Community Hall (the road west here leads back into the hills along Beaver Creek) then meanders around the base of the hills past the derelict church and schoolhouse at Olsen.

For thousands of years, the Indians of the Plains gathered at Head-Smashed-In in the fall for the mass slaughter of buffalo, whose meat they depended on for winter sustenance. They rounded up the herds in the grassy basins of the hills, drove them southwards, them stampeded them over the high sandstone rimrocks which mark the Porcupines' southeastern edge. Many of the animals were killed by the fall and those that survived were quickly dispatched with spears and arrows. The animals were skinned and the meat dried or turned into pemmican in nearby tipi camps. Buffalo jumps were fairly common across the Canadian plains but few were as successful as Head-Smashed-In which was used, almost continuously, for more than three thousand years, and few have survived so well. Many of the other known jumps were looted in the early part of this century, not for the prehistoric artifacts they contained but for the buffalo bones which were scooped up and shipped east in carloads to be used in the manufacture of fertilizer.

Head-Smashed-In is a splendid example of a buffalo jump and the Alberta Government has built a fine interpretive centre here, locating it mostly within the jump cliffs themselves. Inside is a multi-storey experience of the lifeways of the prehistoric Plains Indians and a thorough explanation and re-enactment of the buffalo jump. You can easily enjoy a couple of hours here, then wander around at the lip of the jump and at the bonebeds beneath, where archaeological work is ongoing. The museum makes a splendid finale to a Porcupines road trip, providing a glimpse into a way of life long vanished.

If you are lucky enough to be here at the right time in summer the local Peigan Indians will be holding their annual pow wow in the fields just below the jump. They put up their brightly decorated tipis, erect an open-air pavilion sheathed in cottonwood boughs, don their traditional costumes, bring out the drums, and dance for hours. Spectators are welcome to watch, to join in the Indian games and to sample traditional Indian foods. You can find out the dates of the pow wow and any other museum events by contacting the Head-Smashed-In Centre at 403-553-2731.

Alternative

An interesting loop excursion from Nanton can be made by taking Secondary 533 west across the Porcupines to Chain Lakes Provincial Park and returning via Willow Creek to Stavely. This scenic route takes in the local geological oddity, Magnetic Hill, which appears to defy the law of gravity by permitting a car to roll uphill, and allows for picnics, fishing or an overnight camp at Chain Lakes. To find the return route, one of the loveliest in all the Porcupines, drive back along Road 533 for six kilometres, then branch right (south) along a less travelled road signposted to Stavely. This passes Willow Springs Arena and follows the course of Willow Creek, crossing it three times on one-lane bridges, through beautiful rolling ranch country. It's a narrow, meandering and often dusty road, but one that's a delight to travel. Once you hit pavement again (about 32 kilometres from the Nanton Road) the route becomes a bit confusing: take the next right turn and head east towards the bright red and yellow grain elevators of Stavely. It is a total of 45 kilometres from the turnoff on Road 533 to the junction with Highway 2.

SLOCAN SILVER

If you look at a topographical map of Southern British Columbia, you will quickly see that the grain of the land is strongly vertical. From the Coast Range to the Rockies, the country is broken up into a series of north-south mountain blocks, bony ridges separated by long meandering lakes and deep river valleys. One such valley is the Slocan, a lake-filled gash between the Monashee and the Selkirk Mountains, its waters tributary to the Kootenay River. The valley is quiet now, the lakeshore communities and mining camps in the hills all but deserted but in the 1890s Slocan was a name synonymous with silver.

In the great mountain massif between Slocan and Kootenay Lakes a rich strike of galena (a mixture of silver and lead) was the start of a mining frenzy greater than that of the Cariboo goldrush, and far longer lived. Miners, many of them Americans, swarmed through the hills staking claims and starting mines. Mining camps grew into towns, pack trails to wagon roads; two separate railways fought for hauling contracts from the mines and supply towns fed by paddlesteamers flourished along both lakeshores. The stampede days of silver outroared anything the province had ever seen.

Unlike the Cariboo, where the goldrush days have been immortalized in reconstructed Barkerville, precious little is left of the great days of Slocan silver. The railways have gone and most of the mines have closed for good. Whole communities have vanished; others have settled into a gentle decline, sustained only by tourism. Around them, the mountains are dotted with spectres of an industrial past: mine tunnels and machinery, stamp mills and reduction plants, tailings, railway roadbeds and trestles, tramway scars, old trails, old cabins.

This country road crosses the Slocan mountains from New Denver to Kaslo. It could equally well be driven in the opposite direction but a west-to-east traverse allows you to end the day on Kootenay lake where you can visit an old silver mine, explore some caves or take a dip in the hot springs at historic Ainsworth. Now widened, fully paved

Above and Right: One of the sights of Sandon is this shed door decorated with ornamental ironwork, mostly pieces from old woodstoves.

IDAHO
B.C

The drive and hike up to Idaho Mountain Fire Lookout provide access to wildflower meadows and superb mountain views. Right: hikers along the knife-edge ridge. Below: the flowery trail to the lookout, perched like a pimple on a nose of rock.

Right: The mill at Cody, seen through the windows of a mine sample shed.

Above: Remains of a K&S Railway bridge across Kaslo Creek.

Left: The ruins of Sandon, smashed by Carpenter Creek floods.

trator, with a tramway to the mine workings above. It had its own post office and the K&S railway laid tracks right into town. Little remains today except the ruins of the concentrator, its cedar boards weathered to a beautiful chestnut and with the remains of heavy machinery at its feet. Behind, the scar of the tramway leads up into the hills. Nearby stands a gaunt-eyed multi-storey building and across the road the sagging ruin of a shed still contains a few ore samples.

If you have time after exploring Sandon and Cody, then a trip up to the Idaho Fire Lookout is heartily recommended for it leads eleven kilometres up to the very top of Silver Ridge, passing many of the old mine claims along the way. From the ridge it's a short hike along to the lookout at 2,280 metres and great views down across Slocan Lake to the Valhalla Mountains behind. Before you start, check the condition of the road; snow stays late, arrives early and mud often makes it impassable.

Cross Carpenter Creek and follow the road past the museum and up the hillside. After the first switchback, the road climbs above the valley then levels out, heading back around the shoulder of the mountain before starting its serious ascent. Up to the ridge the road is a mountain one, narrow and with several tight hairpin bends. In places it is definitely one-way. But you don't need a four-wheel drive to make this trip, provided you drive slowly and carefully. It's one of the few roads in the province that come out above the treeline into alpine meadows which in early summer are ablaze with wildflowers. Stop for a picnic in Wild Goose Basin on the way up and don't forget to make the ridge-top walk to the fire lookout.

From Sandon, return the way you came back to the site of Three Forks then turn right (east) along the highway, following Seaton Creek up to the marshy divide. Signs of mining activity and the camps along the valley have all but vanished. Watch for the remains of a trestle bridge at Rambler siding and stop to look for beaver at the ponds by the government sign. Just on the west side of the divide is the site of Zincton, which, as its name tells, was founded on the zinc-rich ores from the Lucky Jim mine which operated, off and on and under different ownerships, until the end of the 1950s. Until the recent demolition of its ruins, Zincton used to be a picturesque place, with the mine buildings spilling down the hillside in a tumble of green paint and rusty roofs. Today, a few concrete foundations and a large wooden ore bin are all that remain. Beaver have taken over the townsite so if you plan to explore, take rubber boots. In mid summer there is usually good picking for saskatoons and huckleberries.

Over the divide are two little lakes, Bear and Fish, headwaters of Kaslo Creek which the road follows all the way down to Kaslo. Here the highway takes over the former roadbed of the K&S railway which once ran right in front of Scotties Hotel at the railway station of Geigerich. From Geigerich, a track leads up to the old minesites of Silver Glance and Summit on London Ridge. At the east end of Fish Lake there is a government picnic site in the trees and just beyond, on the north side of the road, is Fish Lake weather station, part of the highway department's avalanche control system. Temperature, amount of precipitation, humidity, and wind direction and velocity are recorded here twice a day. Higher on the hillside behind can be seen some of the rockwork on the old wagon road, abandoned when the railways deserted the valley and automobile traffic took over the railway right-of-way.

After a lazy start in the lakes, Kaslo Creek gathers strength from its tributaries, picks up speed and rushes through a narrow canyon of black slate, the road squeezed in beside it. Perhaps it was the foaming fury of the creek during spring runoff that suggested the name of Whitewater, the next mining camp along the way. Originally Bells Camp, the townsite became Whitewater when the K&S railway came through and later the name was changed to Retallack after one of the founders of the Whitewater mine. A million dollars in almost solid galena came from Whitewater and other mines above the town yet the flats today are almost empty, green, marshy and jungled with undergrowth. The town suffered from four separate fires, one of which closed down for good the K&S railway whose sagging, moss-covered trestle bridge across the creek still remains at the eastern edge of the clearing. The buildings that line the highway here, red-painted, tin-roofed and abandoned, date from a far later mining operation, that of the Blue Star Mines which operated here until 1967, its workers taking over the bunkhouses and apartments built by Kootenay Belle in the 1940s. A small private residence on the flats is said to be the old town schoolhouse.

A short distance east of Retallack lies the Iron Hand mine. You can see the tunnels if you stop and look up the loose slope to the north of the road. The lower tunnel exits onto what looks like a parapet cut into the rock face but this is the old wagon road again. It's an easy scramble up to the tunnel mouth which has been boarded over. The flats south of the tunnel once housed the dump for

Whitewater mines tailings and waste minerals, including zinc which in the 1890s was considered worthless. Reworked in the 1920s, the discarded tailings produced a rich zinc concentrate with a silver content of 40 ounces per ton.

The log chute beside the road a little farther along was used to load manganese ore directly into railway cars—remember, the present road was built on the right-of-way. Less than a kilometre away a rough road (four-wheel drive needed) goes up to the Buchanan Lookout, eleven steep kilometres distant. Another two kilometres brings you to the ghost town of Nashton and the road up the south fork of Kaslo Creek, (also known as Keen Creek) one of the approach routes into Kokanee Glacier Provincial Park. Nashton grew up at the mouth of Keen Creek in the 1890s, a large and lively shipping centre for valley ores. Today, only a few cabins are left on the grassy flats and the place seems deserted.

From Nashton, it is only eight kilometres downhill to Kaslo, one of the great little mining towns of the Kootenays which has survived. End of steel for the K&S railway and home port for the paddlesteamers on the lake, Kaslo was the supply centre for the Slocan mines and its fortune ebbed and flowed with the price of silver. Kaslo was also the home of peppery Colonel R.T. Lowery, one of B.C.'s great newspapermen, who founded the Kaslo Claim newspaper here, one of eight he started in Kootenay mining camps. The Claim achieved notoriety when it printed half-paid advertisements sideways and unpaid ones upside-down. "Silver, lead and hell are raised in the Kootenays", he wrote, "and unless you can take a hand in producing these articles, your services are not required". The Claim lasted all of 16 weeks.

Kaslo looks back on a long history of disasters—to the great fire of 1894, the hurricane and flash flood a year later. But as long as there was silver in the hills Kaslo rebuilt and prospered. In 1893 it was already a city with a population of 1,500 and 20 grand hotels. Kaslo never went under, even when the mines closed for good. And today much remains of the old silver days: the three-storey Langham Hotel with its row of dormer windows (now a community centre); St. Andrew's Church, built in 1893; the city hall (1898); tree-shaded streets of gracious old homes and a main street with false-fronted shops. And berthed for good on the lakeshore is the S.S.Moyie, one of the last of the lake paddlewheel steamers, now an excellent museum.

South down the highway towards Nelson some 20 kilometres lies Ainsworth, the earliest of all the towns in the Slocan, founded in 1882 beside a natural hot sulphur springs and mostly destroyed by the inevitable town fire in 1898. But there are two original buildings here: the balconied Silver Ledge Hotel and the J.B. Fletcher store, both refurbished and open during the summer months as museums. But most people come to Ainsworth not for the ghosts of the long-gone silver, but for the hot-springs resort. And what better way to end a day of explorations?

In the hills above Ainsworth lie Cody Caves, now within a provincial park. Reached by a rough 13 kilometres of uphill driving, the limestone caves contain 800 metres of safely explorable subterranean passages full of such formations as stalactites and stalagmites, soda straws and moon milk. Conducted tours are available in the summer and the required hard hats, ropes and dependable flashlights can be supplied.

OKANAGAN CIRCLE

The Okanagan Valley, famous for its beautiful blue lakes and dependable sunshine has but one disadvantage: in summer Highway 97 which traces its length from Osoyoos to Vernon is crowded and hectic. Lines of cars and campers harass the travellers, making it impossible to appreciate the golden mood of a leisurely Okanagan summer. Luckily there are country roads, guaranteed to take you wherever you want to go, the slow, beautiful if sometimes dusty way.

This country road leads up the less travelled west side of Okanagan Lake from Kelowna to Vernon and returns to Kelowna through orchards and old steamboat settlements that the highway passes by. Do not expect a waterfront drive, though the route on both sides of the lake traces trails far older than the highway. The shoreline here is steep and rocky and forced even the ancient Indian trails and fur-trade routes onto gentler terrain often high above the lake. To compensate for sparse water access, the views are often stunning. Best of all, even on a summer holiday weekend, traffic will be minimal.

Westside Road begins south of Kelowna's floating bridge. Turn right off Highway 97 at the traffic lights on the top of the hill and follow the signs for Bear Creek provincial park. Okanagan Lake's west shore route was used as early as 1811 by fur-traders and from 1826 until 1847 it formed part of the main north trail of the Hudson's Bay Brigade travelling between Fort Okanogan on the Columbia River and Thompson's Post at Kamloops. A huge train of horses, heavily laden with packs and attendants, made the 450 kilometre journey in about a week; overnight camps were established roughly every 65 kilometres, wherever there was plenty of grass and water for the horses. Westbank where our road begins was one campsite and the head of Okanagan Lake was another. So the first leg of our circular tour retraces roughly one day's journey for the fur-brigades, although by car the distance can be covered easily in an hour.

When the trail up the Okanagan was abandoned by the fur traders in favour of an all-Canadian route over the mountains from Fort Hope, it blazed the way for miners en route to the Cariboo, for stockmen driving cattle north to establish ranches and provide beef to the mining camps and later, for homesteaders. Sections of this historic route still survive, painstakingly searched out and marked by members of the Okanagan Historical Society. (The trail's location has been detailed in an excellent little booklet called "The Okanagan Brigade Trail", published by the Vernon branch.)

Closely following the route of the trail, the first wagon road from Westbank to Nahun was cut through in 1908. Beyond, the steep rock cliff known to fur-traders as the Mauvais Rocher blocked further road access north until 1915 or so when the road to Ewing's Landing was completed. But the west side settlers were not in any case dependent on the road: mail and supplies came in

Right: Spring viewpoint from the Commonage down to Kalamalka Lake, south of Vernon, a glory of green and gold and misty blues.

twice a week by paddlewheel steamer from Kelowna and Okanagan Landing and this explains all the little wharves along the way at places such as Caesar's, Nahun, Fintry and Ewing's.

The West Side road begins unobtrusively through pinewoods then sweeps down to the lakeshore at the old Westside ferry landing and a little bay now filled with log booms. Bear Creek cuts an impressive canyon before it flows into the lake about six kilometres from the highway junction and on its delta, once the site of an Indian village, is Bear Creek provincial park with its large and popular campground and beaches shaded with cottonwoods. It's a good place to stop for there are more than 20 kilometres of easy hiking trails that wind through the canyon and good fishing for mountain whitefish. In early fall, crimson kokanee crowd into the creek mouth, en route to spawning grounds below the waterfall.

Along the road north of the park a sign warns motorists to watch for mule deer and bighorn sheep—the steep wooded country above the lake is ideal for these animals. Open meadows and apple trees at around 14 kilometres are a sure sign that an old settlement is nearby: Wilson's Landing, the first of several former steamboat ports of call, lies by the lake, approachable via Browse Road. Two kilometres farther along, the nurtured grounds of Okanagan Lake Resort spread out along the east side of the road. Much of the traffic will stop here. Beyond, settlement is sparse; the road quiet. In spring the dry pinewoods are bright with balsamroot sunflowers and bedecked in summer with such flowers as wild roses and asters, gaillardias, lupines and salsify.

As you drive along, past the Anglican Camp, keep alert for a gate made from old iron bedsteads which marks the entrance to a Girl Guide Camp. It is here that a long stretch of original fur-brigade trail can easily be located. Park outside the gate and walk down the road, veering south (right) through the second or third campsite. The trail, now used as a bridle path, is well marked. It continues south for several kilometres before disappearing into the brush.

Farther along, a steep road winds down to Caesar's, the second of the old steamboat landing communities, which comes into view across a stretch of open meadowland. At about 25 kilometres, watch for Deighton Road angling down towards the lake. This leads to the settlement of Nahun, once one of the largest of the landings, with several homesteads and a post office. Nearby is the Mauvais Rocher, a steep rock cliff rising sheer from the water, a hazard that blocked the wagon road's progress. Even today, the area poses problems for transportation. The recently relocated and widened stretch of the Westside Road here bears a caution: "Dangerous winding road for 6 km." Another good stretch of brigade trail can be found here close to the eastern edge of Westside Road at .6 kilometres beyond Deighton Road. From here, it goes east then turns south to make its way along the foot of the notorious cliffs, following a much older Indian route along the lake. On the Mauvais Rocher are some faded Indian pictographs and the painter incorporated white veins of quartz on the rock into the designs. From the trail at this historic spot you can look down to the old wagon road leading to the wharf and to the old Deighton home among the orchards of Nahun.

According to Harley Hatfield of the Okanagan Historical Society the trail near the Mauvais Rocher is "perhaps the most spectacular section between Fort Okanogan and Fort Kamloops" and he reports that the place was later known to stockmen as "the Golden Gate" because only a couple of simple bars across the narrow trail here could hold the animals in check.

At kilometre 29, look for a pole corral by a spring on the road's western side. This is believed to be the campsite of botanist David Douglas (after whom the fir is named) who came through the area with an HBC cattle drive in 1833. An old trail leads from the corral down towards the lake to meet up with another long section of well-preserved brigade trail.

The largest delta on this stretch of Okanagan Lake is that formed by Short's Creek, named to honour the first settler. Thomas Short came here in 1883, operated first a rowboat ferry service, then became captain of the first steamship to ply the lake. In 1909 the land around the creek, including the large alluvial delta, was acquired by Captain J.C. Dun-Waters and he called his holdings Fintry after his family's Scottish home. Dun-Waters planted apple trees and raised prize-winning Ayrshire cattle. He also built a gracious stone mansion and his many outbuildings included a unique octagonal barn. For 30 years the "laird" of Fintry brought a touch of European culture to the Okanagan outback—he even imported his own specially labelled Scotch whiskey. Subsequent owners have subdivided the property and summer homes now ring the shoreline of the delta.

Today's West Side road crosses Short's Creek high above the delta and continues north to Ewing's Landing, with its scatter of fields, houses, post-office boxes and roads leading to the lake. Ten kilometres beyond the creek, Bouleau Lake

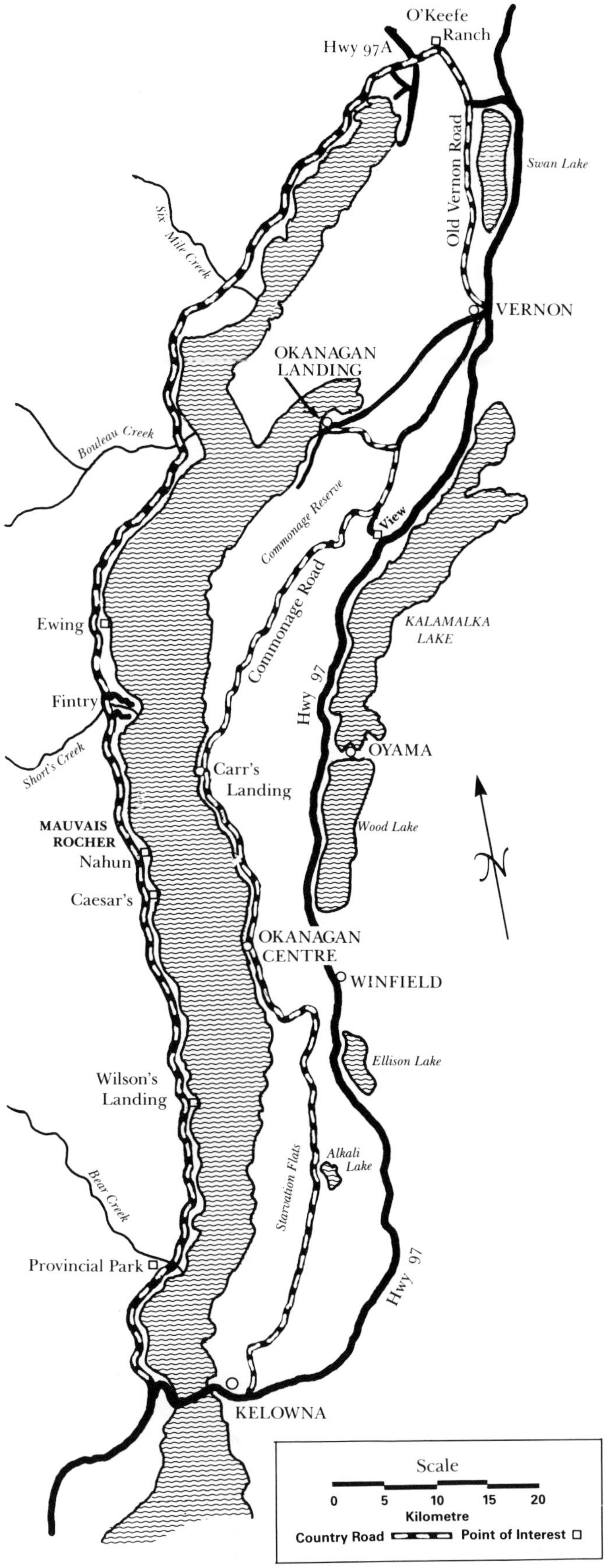

Road comes in from the west and another road heads down to Okanagan Lake Recreation Site. Pause here for further explorations of the old fur-brigade trail. Drive through the campground to the most southerly site. The trail can be found from here, winding parallel to the lake and climbing to reach a rock outcrop. On the rock about 16 metres above the trail is another panel of Indian pictographs painted in two shades of red.

North, as the head of the lake approaches, there is more settlement, more farming activity, even a retirement community at Parker Cove. At 6-Mile Creek there's a gas station and a few kilometres farther an Indian village with a little wooden church. In spring, it sits in a meadow of sunflowers.

West Side Road reaches Highway 97 at kilometre 67; turn right here, passing the O'Keefe Ranch, one of the north Okanagan's most interesting historical spots. It dates from 1867 when Cornelius O'Keefe and Thomas Greenhow, driving cattle to the Cariboo from Oregon, noticed the rich meadowland here and returned to homestead. In 1872 the ranch became the Okanagan post office and later the partners built a store and a church. Today, the settlement at O'Keefe's has been restored to give the public an idea of what life was like in pioneer days. Here is the original tiny log homestead, complete with furnishings, as well as a general store, blacksmith's shop and the pretty little St. Ann's chapel, all connected by a wooden boardwalk. Also here is the later ranchhouse, an elegant 17-room mansion, complete with its Edwardian furnishings. A teahouse and gift shop complete the tourist facilities of a place which is really worth a quick stop. Continue on to Vernon for the second leg of the country tour. If traffic on Highway 97 is heavy, try the old road which follows the north shore of Swan Lake to the city centre. Go through the city and turn right (west) to Okanagan Landing.

The stagecoach route from Vernon to Okanagan Mission (for many years a more important place than Kelowna) climbed the long hill south up to a stretch of grassland country some 600 metres above the lake. This open expanse was known as the Commonage because in 1873 the federal government granted equal grazing rights here to Indians and white settlers alike. Later, the Indians were persuaded to relinquish their claims on these nearly 10,000 hectares in return for the land at the head of the lake and in 1893 the Commonage was opened to settlement. Land sold here for $1.25 an acre and it was quickly taken up. But the homesteaders were in for disappointment. Though it

Opposite Page: Old settlement of Nahun along the west side of Okanagan Lake and the diminutive Chapel of St. Ann at O'Keefe's.

Top: Okanagan orchards in bloom. Above: Balsamroot sunflowers on the hills near the head of the lake. Left: A barn beside the Commonage Road.

looks lush in spring, green and grassy and dimpled with little lakes, the high land on the ridge separating Okanagan from Kalamalka and Wood Lakes was far too dry for farming.

Where it leaves Vernon, the old stage road over the Commonage is known as Mission Road but perhaps it is more interesting to begin this section of the tour at Okanagan Landing. The terminus of the Shuswap and Okanagan Railway which once linked the valley to the main CPR line at Sicamous, the Landing was headquarters for steamship service on the lake. All the CPR steamers were built here, the first, the S.S. Aberdeen, launched in 1893. The ships plied Okanagan Lake until 1935 then their cheerful whistles were heard no more. The last of the CPR ships, the steel-hulled S.S. Naramata, is moored in Paddlewheel Park at Okanagan Landing to remind people of days gone by. Also here is a one-room pioneer schoolhouse, built in 1898, complete with desks and blackboard and moved down from the Commonage in 1973.

From the park at Okanagan Landing drive a short distance south then turn left (east) away from the lake along Okanagan Bench Road which wiggles its way high above the lake. Turn left at the first T-junction, then about 3.5 kilometres farther on, turn right onto Commonage Road. The road coming in from Vernon here is Mission Road and the science fiction dome on the eastern skyline is Vernon's Upper Air Station, a meteorological reporting facility. At another junction about six kilometres farther, turn right, still on Commonage Road, though if it is spring and the balsamroot sunflowers are in bloom detour east here and down towards the highway. From an untroubled vantage point high above Kalamalka Lake, you'll be rewarded with one of the finest springtime views in the Okanagan: the misty blue of water and mountains framed in the green and gold of the hillside.

Commonage Road traverses some fairly open grasslands, interspersed with lakes and stands of trees, with a few old barns and homesteads. One barn, its shingle roof in tatters and its metal wind paddle on the roof a fretwork of shotgun holes, is particularly photogenic. Windpower was once used here to drive some kind of machinery, as you can see by peeking inside the barn. Up here on the grasslands an experiment in irrigation and sewage control is ongoing. Effluent from Vernon's sewage plant, once dumped directly into the lakes system, is treated, mixed with water and pumped up to irrigate and fertilize the crops. Apparently alfalfa grown under this regime is extra rich in protein.

After about 13 kilometres the road leaves the open country and enters a typical Okanagan forest, open and leafy and heady with the scent of pine. It climbs high almost to the spine of the ridge before beginning a swift and sinuous descent onto benchland on the east shore of Okanagan Lake. Here are the familiar orchards and blue lake scenery that one associates with this part of the country—without the clamour of highway traffic. The settlements here are old and slow and peaceful. Detour off Commonage Road to explore Carr's Landing, named for Andrew Carr who homesteaded here in 1895. His orchards thrived in the long sunshine hours of the west-facing benches and they, or their descendents, are still here and the road winds lovingly through them.

A little to the south is a small island, one of the very few in Okanagan Lake. According to Indian legend it is a piece of the Mauvais Rocher itself that rolled down and crossed the lake. Its Indian name, Nahun Wenox, means "child of the rock". Today, Whiskey Island is a nesting place for the lake's colony of ring-billed gulls.

Carr's Road soon rejoins Commonage Road and continues south, very narrow and winding but very pretty, meandering through luscious orchards with the shimmering lake on one side. The countryside has an air of tranquility and timelessness.

The next settlement along the way is Okanagan Centre which was planned as an orchard community in 1907. In 1909, Orchard's Guide to the Okanagan praised the community as "an example of what may be achieved by energy and perseverance, backed by good soil and a perfect climate". With such recommendation there were soon 200 residents, a store, hotel, post office and school, all the essentials of community life. Today, Okanagan Centre seems to have changed little, though the schoolhouse is now a museum. It is serene and beautiful, with a tidy boat harbour and a breakwater, accessible beaches and a backdrop of orchards. You will be tempted to dawdle here and perhaps you should for the best of the day is over.

South of the village, Commonage Road swings inland and climbs steeply east over a forested ridge towards the highway. Turn south along Glenmore Road for the journey into the bustle of Kelowna. Before the days of irrigation, this arid trench, separated from Highway 97 by a rock ridge, was known as Starvation Flats. Today it is green and pastoral, but alas, all too quickly immersed in the suburbs of the Okanagan's biggest city. At 58 kilometres from Okanagan Landing you will have no choice but to join the tourist stream on Highway 97. But you will have peaceful memories.

DISCOVERING THE DEADMAN

British Columbia's Thompson River runs through some of driest countryside in the province: parched craggy hillsides scattered with sagebrush and knapweed, cactus and Russian thistle. In summer, the landscape is hot, dusty and drab; apart from irrigated fields, only small oases in the river's deep trench show any sign of green. In some ways this semi-desert is hostile country: step off the road and you're in a minefield of sharp stones, cactus spines that can pierce the stoutest running shoe, and the ever-present threat of rattlesnakes. Deadman Creek, which flows into the Thompson a little way west of Savona, seems to fit well into this danger scenario. But despite its inauspicious name the creek is a friendly one, providing a respite route north into green ranchlands and cool forested lakes. As a bonus, there are volcanic cliffs beside the creek, brilliantly hued and crazily contorted. And high on the hillside overlooking the valley stand five wind-eroded sandstone hoodoos that are themselves a worthy destination.

Four-wheel drive vehicles can continue up to the headwaters of the Deadman and across the plateau to link up with other backroads. But an ordinary family car can make the trip up at least as far as Deadman Falls. And a side road connection to Cache Creek means you don't have to retrace your steps all the way. From the junction with Highway 1 near Savona to Deadman Falls, returning via the Cache Creek cut-off is just about 140 kilometres, a full day if you allow for picnics and exploration.

Deadman is a fitting name for this creek. Back when B.C. was all Indian country threaded through by a few fur brigade trails, a Mr. Charette, clerk of the North West Trading Company's Fort Kamloops, was found knifed to death at his campsite here. His murderer was never found. The creek was known as Riviere des Defunts, then Knife River and during the goldrush days of the 1860s, as Deadman's Creek.

Before it tumbles into the Thompson, the Deadman carves a crooked and narrow canyon through volcanic bedrock but the valley road bypasses this tough topography and cuts back across the benchland a kilometre to the west (about 4 kilometres west of the Thompson River bridge.) The road is signposted Deadman/Vidette and the first five kilometres are paved, snuggling in close to the creek's cottonwood shade and cool gurgles. Then the valley stretches out into fields and the creek swings away to the west. At seven kilometres the road curves around an Indian cemetery, its crosses neatly whitewashed, and passes the village with its sturdy little church and neat homes. In high summer, the ranch fields are dark blue green with alfalfa and irrigation sprinklers are much in evidence. Farther along, under high cliffs of a brilliant orange brown, the road crosses Criss Creek. Bridging the Deadman at 15 kilometres, the valley pinches in: the road becomes a curving parapet along the river's western edge.

Here, the meadow beside the creek is brilliant

Right: Deadman Indian village and cemetery and Rattlesnake Rocks, colourful but dangerous.

Left: The five sentinels, eroded sandstone pinnacles high above Deadman Valley, can be reached by a short but strenuous hike.

green, a startling contrast to the fire-coloured rocks on the other side. The highest, most highly coloured and most rumpled of these volcanic cliffs are known as Split Rock, for they are deeply fissured and fret, and at one point a deep cleft reaches back into darkness. Rising steeply some 70 metres above the creek, the cliffs are principally volcanic but layered with sedimentary rocks which accounts for their differential weathering. They provide good hunting for agates and petrified wood. Just about opposite Split Rock (at 15.5 kilometres from the highway) a road enters steeply from the west, signposted for Cache Creek. This is our return route.

Geologic oddities of a different kind lie a little farther along this intriguing valley: five gigantic stone hoodoos. Drive north until you come to Deadman Creek Ranch, then stop and scan the hill east of the ranch. From the road the hoodoos about half way up the hillside look insignificant; unless the light is just right you might not be able to see them at all. Only close up can you appreciate their immense size and sculptural beauty, and this requires a bit of a hike. Put on stout shoes and call in at the ranch to ask permission and for final directions. Cross the ranch bridge and head up a rounded hill of petrified yellow sand, then traverse along a rocky slope. It's a hot and strenuous scramble recommended only for the fit, but well worth it. The hoodoos stand nearly 15 metres high in a cluster on the ridge. Eroded pinnacles of rock and clay conglomerate, they are each topped by an overhanging capstone of harder rock which protected the columns when the rest of the unstable ridge weathered away.

Past Deadman Creek Ranch the valley becomes tighter, the rocky hillsides more forested. If you look carefully along the western edges you might notice the remains of an old wooden irrigation flume, one of the few relics of a grandiose scheme to turn the arid benches above the Thompson River far below into orchards. American ingenuity (Charles Barnes) teamed with British wealth (the Marquis of Anglesey) to develop and promote the land. In 1910 the entrepreneurs built a dam on Snohoosh Lake and led Deadman Valley water in ditches and along these flumes (some of them high above the ground on trestle spans) to irrigate the northern benches of the Thompson, a costly proposition. The new orchards went on sale for $350 an acre. Settlers flocked in to buy and a town called Walhachin (Indian for "land of plenty") sprang up across the Thompson River. The Marquis himself built a huge and fancy home here, complete with a swimming pool. Walhachin and the orchards

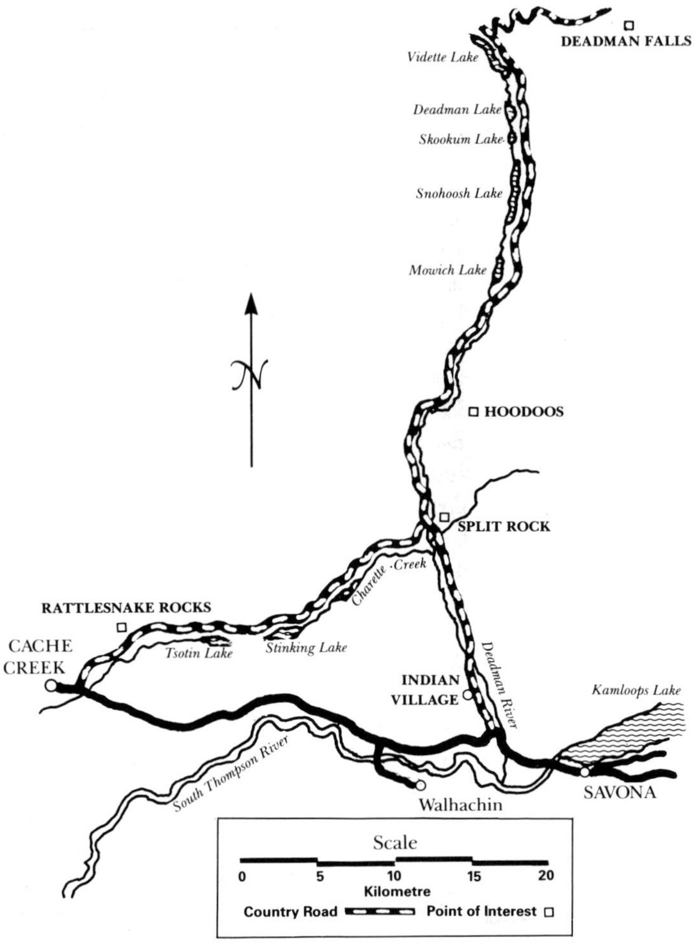

seemed a dream come true. By the time the first crop of Jonathon apples was shipped to market in 1913, corn, tomatoes, onions, beans and tobacco had also been planted on the fertile benchland—all irrigated with water from the Deadman.

But the following year, the trumpets of war called away all but ten of the 107 young men of Walhachin. And a cloudburst washed away huge sections of the irrigation flume on which Walhachin depended. The Marquis had already spent $1.5 million on the scheme and would spend no more. The fruit trees languished for lack of water; the crops failed. And Walhachin faded away. The townsite has barely managed to survive but if you search the sagebrush benches beside the Thompson you might still find a few wizened apple trees blossoming pathetically each spring. The irrigation flume above the Deadman, bleached bone-grey on the hillside, is a fitting headstone to human endeavour.

Past a turning leading to the Sky High fishing camp, the Deadman road cuts through a canyon and crosses the creek. This is the farthest extent of the meadows. North, the valley floor is hemmed in by forests and filled with a string of clear mountain lakes. The first of these is Mowich (Indian for "deer") and a new section of road cuts behind a forested ridge at the lake end, descending to lake level at 35.5 kilometres. A little farther on is Snohoosh Lake, the reservoir for Walhachin water. At its south end you can still find traces of the old wooden cribbed dam, built in 1910. The road used to thread a narrow and twisting course along the lake's eastern bank but today it is broad and straight, with no lake access until a B.C. Forest Service recreation site. Skookum Lake is next in the chain, overlooked by a giant castle of eroded yellow sandstone and edged with waterlilies, then Deadman, where a second recreation site provides good camping. Vidette Lake, perhaps the prettiest of them all, lies just about 50 kilometres from the highway, a well-known fishing spot recently restocked with rainbow and kokanee trout.

The good road this far up the Deadman Valley probably owes its existence to gold. The Vidette mine came into prominence in the 1930s and was touted as "one of the major gold producing areas in the province". A fair bit of gold was produced here—some say the total reached $1 million—but today the buildings here are now a private ranch, all that is left of great expectations.

From the B.C. Forest Service recreation site near the end of the lake the road begins a steep switchback climb onto the Kukwaus Plateau, forested rangeland where in July the wildflowers give a bright display—Indian paintbrush, lupines, geraniums and asters. About ten kilometres beyond the lake, across Joe Ross Creek, take a side road right which leads towards Deadman Falls. Park at a gate and walk a short distance downstream. In spring and early summer, the thunderous noise of the white water dashing over a 50-metre cliff will be enough to guide you. When water levels drop, the falls become quieter but much prettier, reduced to three silvery strands that give it its local name of Three Witches.

Unless you are adventurous and equipped with a sturdy vehicle and a good map, this is the turn around point. Retrace the road back down the valley until you come to Split Rock, then take the Cache Creek Road which follows Charette Creek up into Pass Valley. (Charette, you may remember, was the name of the murdered fur-trader). This part of the trip is well wooded and cool and again there are several lakes. The first of these goes by the Indian name of Cultus, meaning "bad". Reed-rimmed and garrulous with blackbirds, the lake is also home to a colony of bats. A little to the west lies Stinking Lake and if you are there in early summer when the water level is high you might wonder how it earned such a name. The grassy clearing at the western end is just made for picnics; there's a little shingle beach and a great variety of birds—nesting loons, sandpipers, grebes, swallows, kingfishers, flickers and warblers. The pine woods here are open and fragrant, with great tufts of blue-berried juniper, a few blue asters and brown-eyed susans in summer.

From Stinking Lake, the road climbs a bit to negotiate an insignificant pass, then meanders down beside Tsotin Lake, a favourite with local anglers, and picks up Cache Creek for the rest of the way down to the village. Except for a narrow fringe of cottonwood trees and greenery beside the creek, the country here is arid. In early summer if you search the stony sagebrush hillsides you can find the yellow blossoms of Opuntia cactus and the pale pink leafless stars of Lewisia or bitterroot but mostly the mood is sombre. On eroded red volcanic rocks north of the road rattlesnakes bask on the ledges. They are found in great numbers here but will attack only if disturbed. If you brave the snakes, the cliffs are said to be a good source of agates and natrolite.

The Trans Canada Highway just east of the village of Cache Creek lies about 5 kilometres from the rattlesnake rocks (140 from the road's start near Savona). And motorists whizzing by in the heat will have no idea what they have missed.

FROM BULL RIVER TO THE WILDHORSE

Second in popularity only to the restored gold-mining boomtown of Barkerville in the Cariboo, reconstructed Fort Steele near Cranbrook provides its visitors with a rambling experience of turn-of-the-century life in the East Kootenays. The town's half a hundred buildings, some brought in from other sites, some replicas, and others restored originals, have been well detailed and the B.C. parks service runs an outstanding interpretive service, complete with stage-coach rides, an operating steam train, opera house, school and general store, as well as an imaginative programme of street theatre.

The casual visitor is made aware that the restored pioneer town was founded because of the placer mining of gold on nearby Wildhorse River but the sequence of past events tends to be a little obscure. The town itself and even the old police fort in the heart of the town were established a good quarter of a century after the goldrush had gone. And while Fort Steele the historic park is definitely well worth an extended visit, those in search of a truer and more exciting history of the area would do well to travel a different and more difficult road to the sites of the original gold-rush ghost towns of Fisherville and Wildhorse.

Our route begins, not at Cranbrook, the usual jumping off point for Fort Steele, but farther east along Highway 3 where the road crosses the Kootenay River at the mouth of Lake Koocanusa, the sprawling reservoir impounded behind Montana's Libby Dam. (For those interested in name derivations, the lake was named for Koo(tenay), Can(ada) and USA.) Immediately east of the bridge, turn north along the road signposted to Bull River. If you're arriving from the east, this road is a shortcut to Fort Steele, but more important it is a country road, slower, scenic and less travelled, a road that will put you in the right frame of mind for ghost town discovery.

It is only 30 kilometres from the turnoff to the beginning of the Wildhorse Road, but there is plenty to see and at least two stops you will want to make along the way. Bull River, 5.5 kilometres along, was itself the scene of a frenetic though short-lived goldrush back in the early 1860s when a prospector named Bull worked the stream for placer gold. The little town that grew up at the river crossing later turned its hand to lumbering; today, only the lively Bull River Hotel and a few residences remain. If you want to go down to the river to cool your toes or toss in a fishing line there is access by the bridge, one of those solid old-fashioned single lane spans that seem to have been there forever.

On the other side of the bridge lies the Kootenay Trout Hatchery, one of five major installations in the province open to the public for self-guided tours. Beyond, the road curves and climbs until it is high on the shoulders of the Rocky Mountain Trench, the great faultline that scars British Columbia for more than a thousand kilometres along the western edges of the Rocky Mountains. The dominant features of the landscape here are the Steeples, a fluted bare-rock array of peaks, part of the Hughes Range of the Rockies, which prick the western skyline. There are some lovely views across the ranchlands and the open woods of pine, larch and fir, but by far the prettiest panorama is from reflective Peckham's Lake in Norbury Lake Provincial Park which lies about ten kilometres north of the hatchery. The park is off the beaten track, the campsites secluded in the deeper woods and Peckham's Lake sits rimmed by stands of trembling aspen in open grasslands right under those beautiful rock spires. The lake is warm enough for swimming and naturalists will enjoy the wide variety of birds, flowers and mammals to be found here. Deer, elk and bighorn sheep are in the area year-round.

It's only a short drive—less than ten kilometres—from the park to the huge horseshoe bend in the road and the one-lane bridge across the Wildhorse River, one of the few placer gold streams to flow west from the Rockies. As you can see from the huge heaps of piled up gravel and river stones, the Wildhorse has been well worked since gold was first found here back in 1864, only a few years after the discovery of gold in the Cariboo. The gold deposits here were rich and deep, from the gravels along the river edges right down to bedrock; the flakes were big and coarse and nuggets plentiful. Stop by the bridge and look upstream: the sawtooth peak framed in the cottonwoods here is Mount Fisher, the highest peak of the Hughes Range, and it and the shanty town which mushroomed on benchland upstream from the bridge, were named for Jack Fisher, one of the first miners to stake a claim.

By the end of 1864, there were so many miners on the river that Fisherville grew to include six stores, four saloons, a brewery and a motley collection of miner's shacks and tents. Most of the thousand or so inhabitants were Americans, fresh from the played-out goldfields of Montana and California and used to the lawlessness of the American Wild West. For several months the new camp was subject to lynch law; there were several murders, claim disputes, fights, riots and general mayhem. But in August, British Columbia's Gold Commissioner John Haynes arrived, along with a constable, to establish law and order and to register claims, issue mining licences and collect taxes. To the Americans, the taxation system was usurious. Miners had to pay $5 for a three month mining licence, a head tax, customs duty for goods shipped in from the States, plus a hefty two shillings for every ounce of gold exported from Canada. Within a month, Haynes had collected $20,000 for the Colonial Secretary.

It was no wonder that Fisherville was an American camp. Transportation from the south by way of the Kootenay River was far easier and shorter than the tough overland route from the B.C. supply communities of New Westminster and Victoria. All the town's supplies were shipped upriver from Walla Walla and Lewiston, and nearly all the gold left by the same route. To combat this outflow of business and resources, the government in Victoria cast about for an all-British route to the Kootenay goldfields and the following year the Dewdney Trail, that thin line of Canadian civilization threaded through the wilderness from Hope to the flash-in-the-pan 1859 gold strike at Rock Creek was extended all the way to Fisherville. This was a monumental achievement, considering the huge expanse of mountainous, virtually unpopulated terrain it had to cross. Ironically, by the time the trail blazed through to Fisherville, the glut of gold was gone and most of the miners had moved on, to rumours of richer and easier diggings. And the merchants of New Westminster never did get the Wildhorse business they wanted.

Long sections of the original Dewdney Trail to the goldfields and to the site of the first town in the East Kootenays still remain along the Wildhorse River, though followed and partly erased by a modern logging road. Make a sharp right turn onto Wildhorse Road just past the river bridge. The turnoff is marked by a prominent osprey's nest perched on the top of a power pole. The road is well used and a sign at the start indicates if active logging is taking place. Fortunately, the East Kootenay Historical Association has put up signs so that if you watch carefully you can find the remaining sections of the Dewdney Trail which run beside the road at several places.

About six kilometres from the main road, across Brewery Creek, a sign will direct you to a parking lot a little way down a rough road to your right. The first site to explore is the cemetery which lies nearby, a green and leafy place, its many nameless graves edged with picket fences, its wooden headboards indecipherable. In terms of solid remains, this poignant place is all that is left of once thriving Fisherville. In the dying gasps of the gold rush it was discovered that the gravel bench under the townsite itself was rich in gold and the miners did not hesitate to raze the town, moving their shacks higher up to a new townsite known as Wildhorse. To complicate things, the Wildhorse post office, run for many years by miner Dave Griffiths,

Top, left to right: Remains of hydraulic mining near the sites of Fisherville and Wildhorse; St. Eugene Mission church; Storm clouds over the Steeples along the road to Bull River.

Bottom, left to right: Wildhorse cemetery, a green and quiet oasis; Reflections in Peckham's Lake in Norbury Lake Provincial Park; Fort Steele, reconstructed NWMP post and Victorian town.

was known as Kootenay.

Until the excellent work done at this site by the local historical association, it was difficult to make sense of the heaps of rocks, the odd foundations, fireplaces, ditches and flumes scattered throughout this forested benchland. But today, if you park at the cemetery and follow the suggested trails, there are descriptive signs that will explain it all.

While the first flamboyant gold rush was short-lived, there was still much gold in the valley, though it was harder to reach. Larger companies moved in and the local population changed, from entrepreneurs working for themselves to labourers working for wages. Construction of the Victoria Ditch at the huge cost of $25,000 was completed and this brought water for sluicing to 100 new claims high on the river benches. But the glory had gone. And hard winters, disastrous floods and the crippling gold tax were no encouragement to men hoping to get rich quick. Wildhorse was gradually abandoned until large scale hydraulicing operations on the creek some 20 years later started a second momentary flurry.

One can spend a pleasant couple of hours strolling the trails and examining the goldrush sites along the Wild Horse and then it's an easy drive down to the exciting razzmatazz of restored Fort Steele. This settlement was first known as Galbraith's Ferry. It was here that the Dewdney Trail crossed the Kootenay River and here, too, that boats coming upstream from the United States unloaded their men and supplies.

It was the threat of an Indian uprising in the suspicious days following the Riel Rebellion that brought the North West Mounted Police to the area in July of 1887. Several years before, two American prospectors had disappeared in the wilds of the East Kootenays. A year or so later, an Indian named Kapala was charged with their murder and held for trial in the old Fisherville jail. Like a scene from a Wild West movie, a troop of Indian braves led by Chief Isadore stormed the jail and frightened the constable into giving the prisoner up. Bedecked in feathers and war paint, the Indians took Kapala down to Galbraith's Ferry where they whooped it up with drums and dancing. The inhabitants of the tiny settlement were terrified. They knew the local Indians were enraged by the newly legislated reservation system and by the fencing of land they had always used for grazing. Was this the spark to ignite an Indian war?

Word went out to isolated settlers to come to town for safety. A meeting between the Indians and the settlers was to no avail: Chief Isadore refused to surrender Kapala and another suspect,

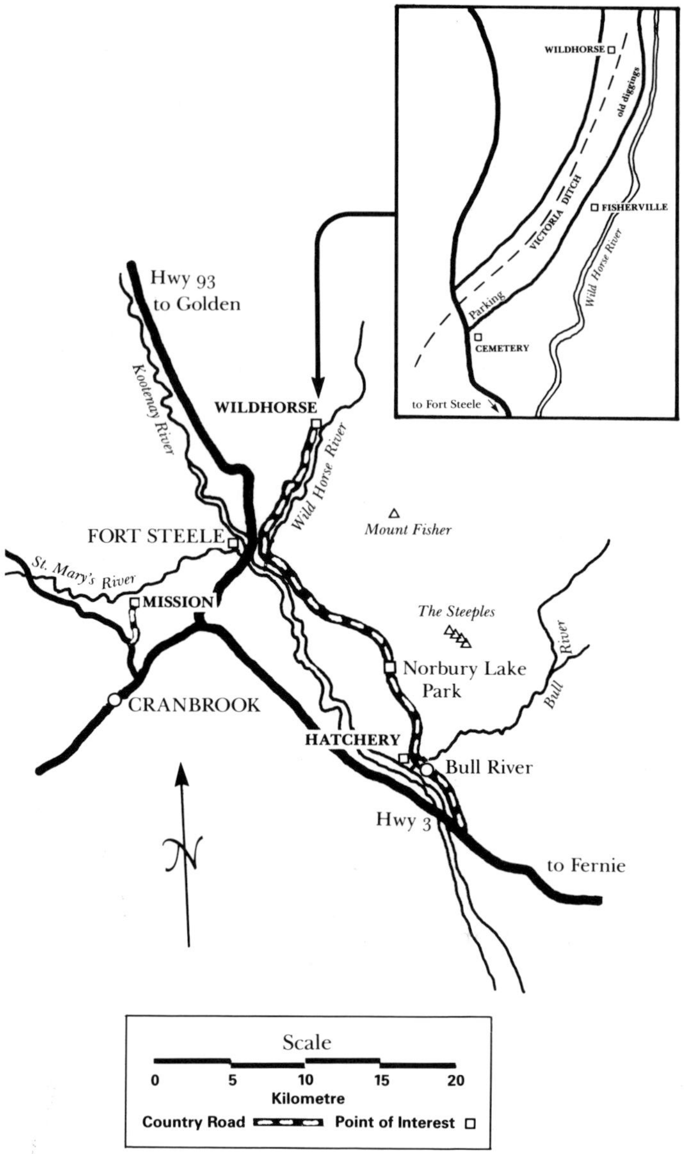

Little Isadore. Word was sent to Victoria and government machinery was set into motion. In July, a contingent of 75 North West Mounted Police under the command of Colonal Sam Steele was sent out from Fort Macleod, Alberta. They rode the brand new Canadian Pacific Railway to Golden, then came down the Columbia/Kootenay rivers, putting their supplies on boats and travelling themselves by horseback along the river trails. Colonel Steele chose to build his police base beside the river at Galbraith's Ferry, where he erected several buildings of sturdy yellow pine logs. He convinced Chief Isadore to surrender the two suspects for trial, dismissed them both for want of evidence and quickly defused the Indian situation. The police stayed for just over a year then packed up and trekked back to Alberta, this time through the

Crownest Pass. And the residents of Galbraith's Ferry changed the name of their town to Fort Steele in the colonel's honour.

Fort Steele slowly prospered. Though the easy gold on the Wild Horse was all but gone, large companies worked with hydraulicing machinery to get at the deeper deposits. Elsewhere in the East Kootenays other minerals were found—silver, galena, copper and coal. The little town on the river was a natural focus for shipping, supplies, entertainment and government agencies. A bridge replaced the ferry and stagecoaches connected the town with the railway at Golden. Population stabilized at around 3,000.

But the town had counted on the Crownest Pass railway coming through to make Fort Steele its main divisional point. When in 1897 the railway crossed the river some 30 kilometres south of Fort Steele and stopped instead at a brand new townsite laid out on Joseph's Prairie, (today's Cranbrook), the town faltered. People and businesses drifted away; the riverboats ceased to call and by 1902 the population of Fort Steele had dwindled to a mere 200. Hotels, stores, churches and schools stood empty and boardwalks rotted. While the town was never completely deserted, it certainly had the look and feel of a ghost town when it was made into a historic park in the early 1960s.

Today, Fort Steele has been reborn, a vintage Victorian frontier town. In summer its boardwalks are lively with tourists, its streets hazy with dust from the stagecoaches, and every morning at nine o'clock the North West Mounted Police raise the British flag over the reconstructed fort. And just a few kilometres away, the ghosts of Fisherville and Wildhorse live quietly in the secluded forests under the stony spires of the Rockies.

Side Trip

If you are at all interested in architecture, you won't want to miss the church of St. Eugene a short drive north from Cranbrook, one of the finest wooden churches in B.C. and one with an interesting history. It was built around the turn of the century with money from a mine.

The Indian mission on the banks of the St. Mary's River, founded in 1874 by the Oblates, included, among other things, a small log church, a school, a farm, a flour mill and a hospital, an outpost of civilization in a country swept through with gold fever. When Father Nicholas Coccola took over the mission in 1887 he encouraged his Indian parishioners to join the prospectors in the hills, for the mission was badly in need of funds. One of them, known only as Pierre, took his advice—and hit pay dirt. The sample of ore he brought back to the mission was almost solid galena, a mixture of silver and lead. The priest and Pierre raced back to the site above the little town of Moyie and staked a claim which they later sold to a mining syndicate for the sum of $22,000.

What Pierre did with his share apart from building a new house is not known. But Father Coccola built two churches, St. Peter's at Moyie and St. Eugene on the mission flats. Later he was asked to build a third church, St. Anthony's, at the nearby new town of Fort Steele. But St. Eugene with its tall spire and fine architectural embellishments was Father Coccola's favourite. He referred to it fondly as "my beautiful Gothic church".

St. Eugene mission school is closed now but the church still stands beside the river. From Cranbrook drive out along Highway 95A to Kimberley but make a right turn (north) almost immediately and follow the winding country road for a short distance alongside St. Joseph's Creek. It's a pleasant drive, a good choice for a summer evening.

DRIVING THE BORDERLINE

Boundaries between nations traditionally follow natural geographical features—rivers, mountain ranges, lakes and hilltops—that are visible on the ground and understandable to the people who live there. But between the United States and Canada the border in the west is defined only by an astronomical line, easily drawn in the imagination or on a map, but geographically nonexistent. Called "topographically absurd", the 49th Parallel of Latitude, an unnatural boundary if ever there was one, was established by the Oregon Treaty of 1846 as a compromise solution between the land claims of Canada and the United States. But there seemed to be no urgency in physically locating this important boundary: work did not begin until eleven years later.

As the surveyors found, pin-pointing an imaginary line on the ground, across rugged mountains, swamps and thick forests, was difficult to say the least. Working against the north/south grain of the country, a contingent of 56 British Royal Engineers plus numerous hired Indians, packers, muledrivers and axemen laboured for four years to survey and cut the boundary line from the coast to the western toes of the Cascade Mountains. Equal forces worked on the U.S. side because it was from the outset a joint commission. Every astronomical survey mark had to be checked and agreed to by the other side. Like joint commissions everywhere, the parties constantly bickered over details: who should report to whom; how to proceed; what were acceptable standards of accuracy; which side was shirking its responsibilities; who should pay for what—irksome details which detracted from the efficiency of the work in hand.

It was monumental work! Remember, this was 1857; there were no roads or railways and only a handful of European settlers. The land was raw. Before the men could start, tote roads had to be hacked out, often high in the mountains or across swamps; bridges built across roaring rivers; camps set up; packtrains organized for supplies; communications established—all in wilderness half the

Above: The glint of snow, the gleam of silos. View from the borderline road to Mount Baker and the Three Sisters.

world away from cosy London and several days' hard journey from the nearest civilization, the stockaded settlement of Victoria. The winters were hard, the summers steaming hot. The mosquitoes were so thick and so ferocious in the Fraser Valley that mules were made blind and men had to cover their heads with bags. Nevertheless, the survey was accomplished and Colonel John Hawkins, in charge of the Canadian operation, could report proudly to the British Foreign Office in London that "for 44.8 miles east of Point Roberts there are 42 iron pillars in place along the boundary line". When, many years later, the accuracy of the original survey was checked with better scientific instruments, little correction was needed. The men had done their job well.

For much of its way through the Fraser Valley the boundary line consists merely of a ditch and a fence (in some places not even a fence) running between the fields. And along most of its length, it is in Canada paralleled by a country road. But west of Yarrow the valley narrows, Vedder Mountain puts its big foot in the way and the ruler-straight line has to force its way through the vertical terrain of the Cascade Mountains. The line is lost to view, except in a few places where it appears as a scar on the forested slopes, and where it crosses Columbia Valley, tucked away south of Cultus Lake. Still the country road, called first Zero Road, then "0" Avenue, then Boundary Road, can be followed, with deviations, all the way from Douglas Crossing almost to Yarrow, a distance of nearly 70 kilometres.

It is, of course, a straight road but it cannot be called dull for it traverses a part of the Fraser Valley that is surprisingly remote, peaceful and lovely. Each season has its advantages: the first flush of spring dandelions give way to the softer gold of buttercups, to lacy stands of cow parsley and moon-daisies, clusters of blue sailors and ripe blackberries; fall brings colour to the scrub alder and the maples and a winter's day will bring the mountains closer, etched in snow. There are market gardens selling bunches of daffodils in April, country stores with brown eggs, farms offering kittens or rabbits, hay meadows, fields of strawberries and raspberries, milk cows knee deep in clover—a wealth of farm sights and sounds. And along the way, you can turn and view the scenery (it's not really very different) across the ditch in Washington State, and count the boundary markers which mark the arduous miles of that historic survey.

Seemingly, not all the boundary markers are in place. When we first made a point of counting them in 1977 there were 20, though I'm sure we missed some in the reckless greenery of the midsummer hedges. A recent quick check found 21, but on previous visits we have tallied as few as 14. Most are sturdy silver-painted obelisks that sit just on the Canadian side of the line. One side of the post is marked Canada, the other, the United States, in case some day you lose your bearings, and each is numbered for the miles east of Point Roberts. The original markers are beginning to deteriorate and recent replacements are skinnier steel poles, not nearly as impressive.

Our country road begins at Douglas, the main truck and bus border crossing south of Vancouver. Just before you reach the customs (about opposite the duty free shop) turn east and zig-zag around a customs parking lot to reach Zero Road running right beside the boundary fence. Almost at once, the road climbs steeply up a little hill. From the top, looking back, the road gleams, the distant sea shimmers and there's a good view to the north across the flat valley to the mountains of Vancouver's North Shore. In late June the salmonberries are ripe and the large white stars of thimbleberry blossoms glow against the bright green of their maple-shaped leaves. Behind them, the forest looms darkly, the only barrier between Canada and the U.S. You must watch carefully to find the boundary mileposts in the bushes here. The first we found recently was Number 6, then Number 7 at the intersection with 184 Street, then, spaced roughly a mile apart, Numbers 8 to 26.

Surprisingly, while the boundary line through the mountainous country between Hope and the Rockies was surveyed relatively easily, the stretch from Semiahmoo Bay at today's White Rock to Sumas caused all sorts of problems, at first because of disagreement with the U.S. surveyors over procedures and standards, then because of the thick, swampy forests. When the British survey crew arrived they found the Americans had started a season earlier and "had cut a track through the woods from Semiahmoo to Sumas but . . . it is of little use as indicating the boundary, both from error in direction and from the extreme difficulty of making a way through such dense and difficult forest land." This is an excerpt from one of the official reports by the British Boundary Commission. The correspondence, day-to-day reports on the survey and the meetings with the Americans, is worth reading if you have a stomach for bureaucratic verbiage. Far easier to digest is the diary of commission secretary, Charles Wilson, who reports on the social life and conditions, as well as the daily routines. The diary was edited by George Stanley and published as "Mapping the Frontier between

British Columbia and Washington."

From these reports, it appears that the British boundary team established a camp at Sumas Prairie in August, 1858 and sent survey crews off in both directions. The initial work on this stretch of the boundary proved faulty and in 1861 the crew had to return "to rectify the direction of the boundary line . . . and to fix iron monuments along that portion". The iron monuments which had to be transported from England were a British idea. The Americans baulked at the cost, preferring to build stone cairns from materials on hand. But the British persisted and eventually the monuments, which originally marked every mile from the sea to the western base of the Rockies, were supplied and installed solely at the expense of the British government.

Back in 1977, one of the markers showed the amazement with which foreigners view the casual nature of the Canadian/U.S. border. Written on it were the words: "Is this all there is? Where are the barbed wire and the guard dogs?" Officials have since painted over this interesting graffiti. A pity—it was a monument in itself.

After Monument 19, "0" Road intersects Highway 13 crossing into the United States at Aldergrove/Lynden (there's another marker on the road here) and detours around the duty free shop and Canadian customs before resuming its eastward direction. On the other side of the border ditch a road parallels the Canadian one (both are here called Boundary Road) and the valley opens up to the south with views of Mount Baker. The valley's lush strawberry and raspberry fields begin around Monument 21, their neat rows converging on the horizon, alternating with hayfields and cow pastures, farmhouses, milking sheds, silos and greenhouses. The land here is fertile, today some of the most expensive farmland in Canada. But in 1902 when the Settlers' Association of B.C. published a calendar to promote immigration and advertise land prices, land hereabouts went for $20 and $30 an acre.

At Bradner Road sits one of the new style steel markers which bear no numbers. Marker No. 23 is near Fishtrap Creek and there's another new marker near Mt. Lehman Road, which is about 24 kilometres east of the Douglas Crossing. At Townline Road, another kilometre or so along, the boundary road comes to an end because a large gravel operation, and the northern tip of Judson Lake lie in the way. Judson Lake sprawls across into Washington State and is a favourite area with valley bird watchers for its concentrations of migrating waterfowl. It is also famous as the only place in B.C. and Washington where the little blue heron has been sighted. If you stand at the corner and look east you can see the border, marked only by a fence, striding towards the lake.

Drivers intent on following the borderline must turn north and follow Townline through the raspberry fields and packing plants (Clearbrook calls itself "the Raspberry Capital of Canada") to its intersection with Huntingdon Road, here the closest east-west road to the border, at the edge of Abbotsford Airport. Follow Huntingdon east through the community of South Poplar into South Abbotsford, skirting Matsqui prison. You're heading now for the well-travelled Highway 11 leading south to Huntingdon/Sumas border crossing, where on a busy Sunday you might very well find a traffic jam. You might want to end your explorations of the valley here and speed back to Vancouver on nearby Highway 1. But there is more of the boundary to follow, and an interesting drive along the valley's southern edge will bring you to Yarrow. Join the traffic going south on Highway 11 and make a left turn onto 2nd Avenue just before you reach Canada customs. This road bends around to cross the B.C. Hydro Railway line (formerly the B.C. Electric) and brings you onto International Boundary Road. To the east, you can see the border slash climbing the slope of Vedder Mountain.

One of the biggest obstacles to settlement in this part of the Fraser Valley was Sumas Lake, a shallow, marshy tract that covered almost 15,000 hectares of potentially prime farmland. The B.C. Electric Railway routed its line south of the lake on slightly higher ground, following the example of

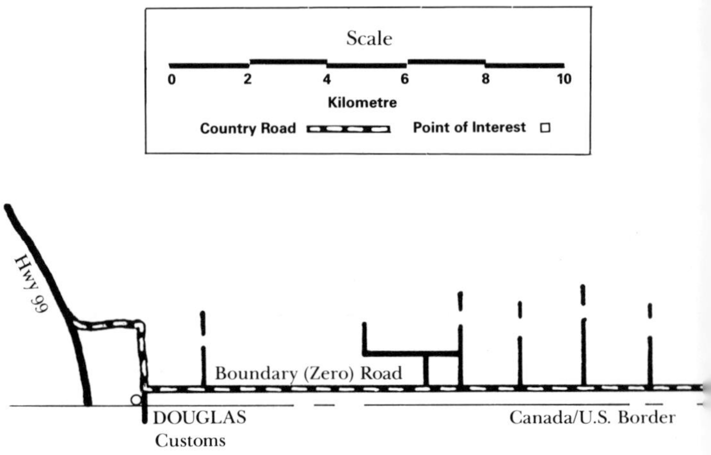

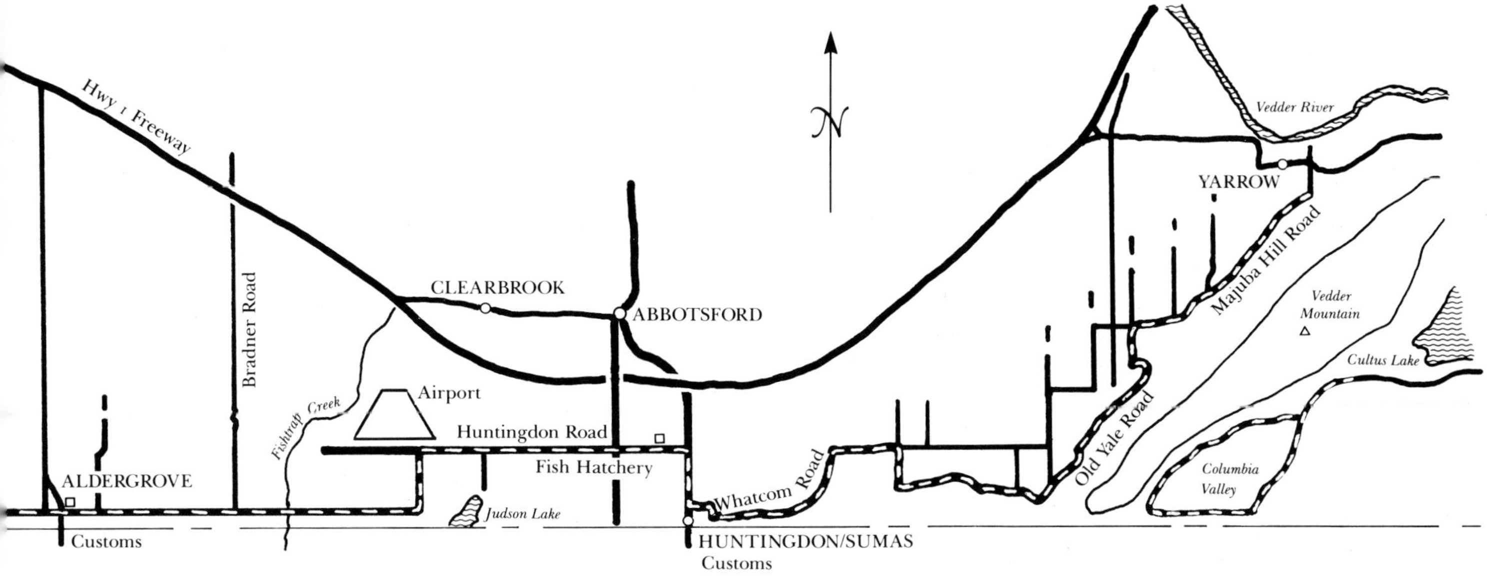

the Yale Road, the first wagon road from Fort Langley. The few settlers in the area had to confine their holdings to the high ground ridges around the lake, a system of dry-point farming which is still evident in the area today: all the older homesteads and barns are built on knolls or treed ridges.

It was Sumas Lake and the surrounding swamplands that gave the British boundary surveyors their worst moments. Here they had their main depot, consisting of one small log house, and Charles Wilson wrote in his diary that it was "the most beautiful place I was ever in". Unfortunately, the area was plagued by mosquitoes and "sand-flies" from mid-June until September. "The mosquitoes have now regularly set in," wrote Wilson. "It is perfect agony performing even the regular actions of life. Washing is perfect torture, they settle en masse upon you perfectly covering every portion of the body exposed. We sit wrapped in leather with gloves on and bags round our heads and even that cannot keep them off; none of us have had any sleep for the last two nights and we can scarcely eat, exposing the face is such a painful operation, day and night no peace". Some of the men came down with malaria and two of the mules were blinded by insect bites.

Between 1920 and 1924 the federal government drained Sumas Lake as part of a massive flood control programme in the Fraser Valley. A canal was dredged through the middle of the old lake bed and numerous ditches and diversion channels dried up the marshy swamp in which Wilson had once floundered his canoe. Dykes protected the area from future floods and the land was opened to settlement.

The countryside east of Huntingdon is rich dairy land; the barns are expansive, the outbuildings neat, the silos tall. Black and white Holstein cows munch in the meadows. The farmers here, safe behind the dykes, are mostly of Dutch origin and choose Holsteins because they give the highest milk yield and the lowest fat content. In 1977 there were two boundary markers, Numbers 32 and 33, along this stretch of the boundary road, the latter beside the Sumas River where the Whatcom Trail crossed into Canada. Here Boundary Road peters out and the way turns to follow Whatcom Road whose winding course would tell you of its foot trail origins even if you had not guessed. Whatcom Road twists through one of the loveliest farms in the valley, with all the barns and outbuildings painted a spanking white and with white-railed fences on both sides of the tree-shaded road.

The boundary route is finished now, apart from glimpses of the survey slash as it slices into the hills, but our route from here to Yarrow, keeping as close to the border as one can, is worth your time. Cross the railway again, heading east on Vye Road into the flatlands, once marshes teeming with wild duck. Watch for Lamson Road which ducks underneath the old BCER, here built up on an embankment, and take a short side trip down towards the border through a slice of the valley, cut off by the railway, which seems extra quiet and pastoral. Lamson joins Old Yale Road just north of the boundary and this heads east again, taking a winding course between the flat meadows of the valley and the abrupt edge of the mountains, keeping as high as possible above the swamps of old Sumas

24

Looking north from Boundary Road through strawberry fields to mountain snows.

Mount Baker dominates the rural landscape along the border.

Far Left: The border slash runs straight and true through the mountains east of the Columbia Valley.

Left: One of many boundary markers along the borderline road. Distant Mount Baker looks down on Washington State raspberries.

Far right: The long Canada/U.S. border is mostly unguarded; graffiti expresses incredulity.

Lake. All side roads leading enticingly south to the actual border dead-end in farmer's yards but you can see the border slash climbing up Vedder Ridge to cross over into Columbia Valley, south of Cultus Lake.

Old Yale Road soon becomes impassable for traffic and you must turn north on Maryann which ducks under the railway again and joins Powerhouse Road. Keep east on Powerhouse, heading straight for Vedder Mountain. On the slope here stands what at first glance could pass for an elegant Palladian mansion of pale marble, its windows decoratively arched. In reality it is the old Sumas Power Station, made of cement, which supplied electricity to the railway. Old Yale Road makes another brief appearance here, crosses the tracks and heads along its original high course along a forested parapet, but it is not recommended for autos any more.

Keep going along the country roads, always staying as close to the border as possible, on Wells Line, then on Campbell Road. Turn right on Belrose uphill across the railway tracks. The plateau above was originally known as Majuba Hill (named for a famous Boer War battle) and, high above the valley floods, it was settled early. Belrose joins Old Yale Road again as it climbs the hill and today the road is known as Majuba Hill Road. This leads most pleasantly up into the forest clearings around the early homesteads and gives good views of the valley below. After about four kilometres Majuba Hill Road makes a sharp bend and heads north into Yarrow. At the bend is tiny Majuba Heritage Park, a grassy triangle with a cairn marking the site of the Old Yale Wagon Road. A portion of this historic road strikes off eastward from the park and makes an interesting walk.

To reach Yarrow, which was first settled by a group of Mennonite families in 1928, turn left when you reach Yarrow Central Road. The pleasant single-street community with several small stores and a good little restaurant is within very easy reach of Highway 1 for a fast route back to Vancouver.

Sidetrip

There is another stretch of road that parallels the border near here and there are (or there used to be) two markers to find. To reach the road, you must turn east instead of west on Yarrow Central. The road soon hits the base of the mountains, turns into Vedder Mountain Road and leads to Vedder Crossing, site of the Canadian Armed Forces Base and the excellent little museum of the Royal Engineers—the "sappers" who built many of B.C.'s earliest roads, surveyed many of the first towns—and worked on the boundary survey.

Before the Vedder Bridge, turn south at a traffic light and drive to and through the resort community of Cultus Lake where the British Boundary surveyors had one of their camps. Beyond Cultus Lake lies the Columbia Valley. The road goes south down one side of the valley, turns and runs parallel to the boundary, then comes back, making a handy little loop tour, with a couple of boundary markers to look for and grand views of the border slash running straight as a die through the rugged Cascade Mountains.